COMPASSIONATE ENERGIES DANCING THE COSMIC DANCE

Reflections
of an
Old Priest
on the
Cosmic Dimensions
of the
Spiritual Journey

Larry Hein, S. J.

Copyright © 1996 by
John Lawrence Hein, S.J.

February 20, 1996
New Orleans, Louisiana

First Printing 1996
Second Printing 2001

Library of Congress
Catalog Card No. 96-95016

ISBN 1-57579-039-4

All Rights reserved.
No part of this book may be reproduced or translated without the previous written permission of the author which will be freely given.

Imprimi Potest: R.P. Edward B. Arroyo, S.J.
Praep. Prov. Neo Aurelianensis
Sociatatis Jesu

Printed in the United States of America
PINE HILL PRESS
4000 West 57th Street
Sioux Falls, S.D. 57106

*To Norma and Lawrence, my parents
and Kenneth, my brother,
for their courage, strength, love,
faith, humor and mischievousness.*

and

*To Harry Martin, S. J.
who once wrote
of us Old Crocks
"Just possibly we do
less harm and more good."*

and

*To Barbara Erichson
a
Most Courageous Compassionate Energy,
the
Midwife of this Baby*

Contents

Preface vii
Acknowledgments ix
Introduction xi

I. THE ONE AND THE MANY DANCING
    THE COSMIC DANCE 1
    A. The One 1
    B. The Many 3
    C. The Relationship Between the One and the Many 6
    D. Images Formed by Perception of Cosmos 9

II. ENTER ANGELS AND OTHER COSMIC
     ENERGIES 13
    A. Introducing Clarissa 15
    B. Why Missy Is With Me 16

III. MISSY SPEAKS ON RELIGION 21
    A. The Purpose of Religion 21
    B. Misunderstandings Can Cause Wars 23
    C. Invitation to Changing Images 24
    D. Why Such Resistance to Change 26

IV. DEATH IS AN ILLUSION 35

V. I AM THE LIGHT OF THE WORLD 37
    A. Images of the Transcendent 37
    B. Cosmic Irreversible Transitions—Passovers 40
    C. Images Again 43
    D. Sins 44
    E. Sin/Darkness—Missing the Mark 46
    D. Salvation by Christ the Light of the World 49

VI. EXERCISES FOR COMPASSIONATE ENERGIES 55
  A. Principle and Foundation 56
  B. Sin/Darkness on Planet Earth 60
  C. Sin/Darkness in My Persona 78
  D. Annunciation and Incarnation Year Zero A.D. ..92
  E. Annunciation and Incarnation in the Year 199? .95
  F. Reflections on the Kingdom of God 101
  G. The Call to Compassionate Presence 105

Appendix 107
Recommended Reading 111

Note: All Biblical quotations are from the 1966 edition of the Jerusalem Bible, except where noted.

Preface

There is the saying that fools rush in where angels fear to tread. Old fools don't rush in, they just keep stumbling along.

These musings rose out of a need to clarify for myself, and anyone with whom I may be journeying, the images and movements which have taken place within me and others in the past twenty-five years or more. I am speaking about the images of God, of Human, of the Cosmos, of Sin and Salvation. These are indeed rather large dimensions of the human experience. The only qualification I have for writing about them is that they have occupied a great deal of my energy, both for myself and for those who have invited me to accompany them on their spiritual journeys.

I have created exercises for compassionate energies, spirits, souls, cosmic consciousnesses, sparks of the divine—all participating in the evolutionary process of the Cosmos; more specifically, the evolutionary process of Planet Earth and even more specifically, the evolutionary process of the human species.

The exercises are part VI of these musings. You may wish to skip all of the musings and go directly to the exercises. If you do, however, you will miss a lot of playful dancing in the wisdom of the ages! ! ! !

As a Jesuit I have constantly had the Spiritual Exercises of St. Ignatius of Loyola as the touchstone or backdrop from which I am present to others. Therefore, the exercises I present follow the same schema. The changes are in the Images of God, Human, Sin, Salvation, which may be nothing more than changes in my perception of God, Human, Sin and Salvation.

My editor has asked me to make up a glossary of terms which I use. I have great compassion for her in her desire to save me and make some sense out of my babblings. I thank her and have compassion for her and for all who attempt to follow me in this inner and outer galactic journey-dance. Somehow, the terms change or simply do not allow themselves to be pinned down to precise definitions. Perhaps the more we dance in wonder and wander in the diaphanous mystery, the more we will be caught up in the continual birthing of galaxies of which we are whatever we are.

Acknowledgments

I acknowledge all of the angels who have busted their metaphorical butts taking care of me for the past 75 years. There are also the many embodied angels who have loved me, encouraged me, and enabled me in the Passover step of the Cosmic Dance. Fellow Jesuits have encouraged me by the uniqueness of who they are—especially Harry Martin, S. J. Particularly I am grateful to Don Martin, S. J. who helped me make the transition from a Tridentine/Vatican I mentality to the openness beyond Vatican II. Religious of the Cenacle have inspired me by their living in the mystery of God's goodness and inviting others to do so. I am grateful also to Sr. Jane Pellowski, M.M.S., who introduced me to the art of dreamwork and to the works of Anthony deMello and to Thomas Merton's writings on Zen and Taoism. Sally McPhillips introduced me to various authors such as Brian Swimme, Brian Weiss, and Deepak Chopra. Thanks Sally. I am grateful to Robert Baker, Ph.D., who introduced me to hypnosis. Thankful I am to those who introduced me to guided imagery. Thanks also to Stephanie Dodge and Patricia Ann Scott who introduced me to various massage therapies, acupressure and cellular energetics. To each and all I am very grateful for they have invited me into transition, the Passover step of the Cosmic Dance.

I am also grateful to Lake Pontchartrain, to the trees on the Cenacle grounds, to the rabbits, the squirrels, the nutria, to all the birds and especially little owl. They have all supported me in this movement.

However, this book would never have been without the presence of "Henry," my prostate cancer, inviting me to wonder and wander, and the help of "Harold" the computer loaned to me by Barbara Erichson who—along with Rosalie Ambler, though separately—very frequently and patiently listened to and challenged me in my musings, making it easier for me to process them. To them and to many others I am grateful for love, encouragement and compassionate presence. I am deeply indebted to Karen and Monroe Laborde for their questioning and suggestions.

Very special thanks to Karen Laborde for endless hours of editing and typing the manuscript. Needless to say it could only be done with much compassion and love.

The cover design is by Laverne Parfait. Thanks much for your enthusiastic play. At least this little book has great looks.

Finally, I am deeply grateful to Mindy Malik for her enthusiastic encouragement, love, and support in the publication of the manuscript. Mindy, I thank you.

Metairie Cenacle
July 31, 1996
Feast of St. Ignatius Loyola

Introduction

When I was ordained a priest in 1951 the theology of the time as I perceived it imaged God as the Creator, Ruler and Judge of the Cosmos. The Cosmos was viewed very anthropocentrically and God was viewed anthropomorphically.

Human was imaged as a creature composed of body and soul. The purpose of human was to know, love and serve God and thus to be happy with God forever in heaven.

These humans were basically to follow the Ten Commandments and the six precepts of the Roman Catholic Church. If they were to go against any of these in a serious way, with sufficient reflection and full consent of the will, they committed a mortal sin. Should they die without being sorry for this sin they would be condemned to everlasting hellfire.

Sin was imaged as a free act of will on the part of human by which human transgressed one of the laws of God or of the Church. Since all sin was supposedly an act against God, it terminated in God Who is infinite. Thus the sin became infinite, and human, being finite, could not make satisfaction to the infinite God. God's infinite and perfect justice demanded satisfaction.

God in his infinite love for man gave his only begotten son, Jesus Christ, to die for our sins, both the original sin of Adam and Eve and any actual sins that we ourselves have committed. Thus was the infinite justice of God satisfied and we were redeemed. Since He was both God and man he could redeem us. He was the sacrificial victim on the cross on Calvary. This is called a propitiatory sacrifice.

This prevailing theology of the time is still part of our dogmatic tradition. For many it seems to be the center of our dogmatic tradition and the only acceptable teaching of the Church.

As for the Cosmos, intellectually we may have been up to the heliocentric image of the Cosmos, but in our religious thinking we were still back with the Sumero-Babylonian image of the flat earth, the heavens above, and the underworld beneath us, all of which was encircled by the ocean.

These are very succinct statements, possibly rather negative and harsh and over-simplified. However, I think they were the bottom line for most priests and the vast majority of the laity at the middle of this century.

In the first five parts of these musings I share with you the thinking and imaging to which I have come over the past thirty-three years. During this time there was the Second Vatican Council, which opened the windows and let in fresh air. Also during this time the focus of my ministry was giving retreats to groups and individuals following the Spiritual Exercises of Ignatius of Loyola. I was also involved in Ecumenism, Marriage Encounter, the Charismatic Movement and so on.

This background invited me to look at what I perceived was the theology supporting the Spiritual Exercises—namely, the redemption of human by a propitiatory sacrifice, i.e., Jesus Christ is the victim on the cross, and the Father is the One propitiated. The focused imagery of the Exercises included the Kingdom of God with Christ the King to be generously followed by all loyal subjects. To do this we must always be aware of our inordinate attachments and free ourselves of them in order to follow the King. This over-simplified perception did not fit well, but it was mine.

Then one day I read one of Teilhard de Chardin's letters to his friend, Pierre LeRoy, in which he said that he found the Cosmology and hence the Christology of the Exercises childish, and that they should be offered with new imagery based on the understanding of Cosmogenesis. I do not flatter myself to think I have done what Chardin had in mind. Rather, I simply share the insights and the imagery that have come to me in dialogues with many friends, from readings, and from just plain walking with my girlfriend, Lake Pontchartrain.

From many sources—especially Chardin's letters, some of Joseph Campbell's more popular works on Mythology, and Brian Swimme's book on the Universe—I came to appreciate that we live in a Cosmos of swirling galaxies of which ours is but one and Planet Earth is a very small bit in the midst of billions. I also came to appreciate that religions on Planet Earth are rooted in the imagery of *homo sapiens* attempting to express their experience with the Ineffable Transcendent. Both individually and collectively we want to have some metaphorical structure and medium in which and through which to relate to the same Ineffable Transcendent.

I came to see that the structures of Religion—definitive Creed, Code and Cult—were very necessary to most individuals. The structures within which they grew up and within which they learned and practiced were real supports throughout their lives, particularly in times of crisis. If the structures were questioned, their security was threatened and they could become very angry.

Over the years I became aware that for many individuals religion, instead of being the support system it was meant to be, had become a burden. Religion, the definitive Creed, Code and Cult, becomes a burden when individuals allow themselves to be determined by this support system rather than being supported by it on their spiritual/faith journey. Then religion becomes a bondage rather than a help.

All humans on the planet are invited to be on this spiritual/faith journey. Their religions, the support system for individuals and for the collectivity, may differ but ultimately the movement—the spiritual journey toward the Transcendent within—is the same for all.

PART I
The One and the Many Dancing the Cosmic Dance

THE ONE—The Source from which the many are.

THE MANY—the ten thousand things of which the human species is one.

Playfully and daringly, and with all due respect to the many scholars in all the disciplines of sacred theology and spirituality, I celebrate a Cosmic image of Sin, Salvation, the Lordship of Jesus the Light of the world—a superb Cosmic Dancer. I also celebrate the Prodigality of a passionately loving Mother/Father/Evolver God who invites each of us to participate in the creatively ongoing process of Cosmogenesis by simply being the wonder that each of us is. I call this the Cosmic Dance of the One and the many; the Transcendent and the many of which each of us is one.

The One

What is this Transcendent Mystery?

The Chinese call it the Tao. I am told that frequently when the Prologue of St. John's gospel is translated into Chinese the symbol for the Word is the Tao. It is the Way or the Source from which all comes. The Tao te Ching very definitely says that if the Tao is expressed or named, then what is expressed or named is not the eternal Tao. The unnamed is the source of heaven and earth. When we remain in the state of no desires we may experience the Mystery. When we are desiring we experience the manifestations. Both desiring and not-desiring are values in the human condition. It is well that neither supersede the other. Then we may experience the Transcendent Mystery.[1]

The Mystery is that which cannot be imagined, conceptualized or worded. It is the nothingness and the no-nothingness which permeates every atom of the Cosmos and is the Source of all that is. Physicists who study quantum physics speak in this manner when they say it is just as much a mystery to them as it is to us to whom they may try to talk about it. They speak about protons jumping in and out of existence in atoms, and they acknowledge that they do not have the slightest clue as to how or why this happens.

"In the language of physics, we call it quantum fluctuation," writes Brian Swimme, a noted quantum physicist:

> "Elementary particles fluctuate in and out of existence..A proton emerges suddenly...it simply leapt out of no-nothingness. There was no particle, then there was. I am not speaking here of the manner in which mass and energy can be transformed into one another. I am speaking of something much more mysterious. I am saying that particles boil into existence out of sheer emptiness. That is simply the way the universe works.
>
> I say no-nothing-ness. Or emptiness. But this only reveals the limits of language. We are here approaching an Ultimate Mystery, something that defeats our attempts to probe and investigate. There was no fireball, then the fireball erupted. The universe erupted, all that has existence erupted out of nothing, all of being erupted into shining existence.
>
> What I would like you to understand is that this plenary emptiness permeates you. You are more fecund emptiness than you are created particles. We can see this by examining one of your atoms. If you take a single atom and make it as large as Yankee stadium, it would consist almost entirely of empty space. The center of the atom, the nucleus, would be smaller than a baseball sitting out in center field. The outer

---

[1] Cf. *The Tao te Ching* chapter 1.

parts of the atom would be tiny gnats buzzing about at an altitude higher than any pop fly Babe Ruth ever hit. And between the baseball and the gnats? Nothingness. All empty. You are more emptiness than anything else. Indeed, if all the space were taken out of you, you would be a million times smaller than the smallest grain of sand.

But it's nice knowing we are emptiness, for this emptiness is simultaneously the source of all being. You see?"[2]

Where is the Transcendent Mystery, the Tao, the One dancing the many? Everywhere and nowhere for it is neither temporal nor spatial. For centuries the ancients of China, India, and the West have talked about the nothingness from which all is.

There is a wonderful story in the Chadogya Upanishad c 900 BC, India. The father, Aruna, tells his son, Svetaketu, to bring him a fig and to divide it. He divides the fig and then the seeds in the fig. When he finds nothing Aruna tells him that the finest essence which he does not see is the source of the fig tree, the source of the world, and that is what Svetaketu is.[3]

We are reminded of what St. Paul says to the Greeks, "In God we live and move and have our being. We are all children of the one God" (Acts 17:28). St. Paul simply puts this tremendous mystery in anthropomorphic terms.

The Many

Who or what, then, are the many?

In his introduction to the *Bhagavad Gita* Aldous Huxley writes, "At the core of the Perennial Philosophy we find four fundamental doctrines:

---

[2] Reprinted with permission from *The Universe is a Green Dragon*, by Brian Swimme, Copyright © 1984 Bear & Co., Santa Fe, N.M. p. 35-38.

[3] cf. Joseph Campbell, *Historical Atlas of World Mythology*, Vol II (New York: Harper & Row, 1988) p. 84

First: the phenomenal world of matter and of individualized consciousness—the world of things and animals and men and even gods—is the manifestation of the Divine Ground within which all partial realities have their being, and apart from which they would be nonexistent.

Second: human beings are capable not merely of knowing about the Divine Ground by inference, they can also realize its existence by a direct intuition, superior to discursive reasoning. This immediate knowledge unites the knower with that which is known.

Third: man possesses a double nature, a phenomenal ego and an eternal Self, which is the inner man, the spirit, the spark of divinity within the soul. It is possible for a man, if he so desires, to identify himself with the spirit and therefore with the Divine Ground, which is of the same or like nature with the spirit.

Fourth: man's life on earth has only one end and purpose: to identify with his eternal Self and so come to a unitive knowledge of the Divine Ground."[4]

The many include all that are not the One or the Divine Ground or the Transcendent. Yet the many are in the One and the One is in the many. I can play only with one small species of the many—*homo sapiens*—on Planet Earth.

> *May they all be one.*
> *Father, may they be one in us,*
> *as you are in me and I am in you,*
> *so that the world may believe it was you*
> *who sent me.*
>
> John 17:21

The physical of human is this temporary phenomenon which we call the "body" animated by spirit, soul, the spark of the Divine. It is something that is very much in flux and although it seems to be a separate entity, is very much a part of the movement of the Cosmos. "We are like

---

[4] *Bhagavad Gita* (New York: The New American Library, 1951) p. 13.

the stars...thermodynamic systems...vortices in turbulent nature," writes Fr. David S. Toolan S.J., in his article "Nature is a Heraclitean Fire" (whose title he borrowed from Gerald Manley Hopkins' poem, "That Nature is a Heraclitean Fire and of the Comfort of the Resurrection"). In an introduction to Fr. Toolan's article, Fr. John Padberg S.J., notes that "The Greek philosopher Heraclitus is supposed to have called the soul 'a spark of the substance of the stars.'" In this way of thinking and imagining, human is simply a dimension of this Heraclitean Fire, a dimension of the One.

Wondering about the Universe emerging from the "Big Bang," Fr. Toolan writes:

> "What to make of this? The point, as Hawking phrases it, is that 'the odds against a universe like ours emerging out of something like the Big Bang are enormous. I think there are religious implications.' From this angle, it begins to look as if human beings, for all their distinctiveness, are modes of being of the universe. As Thomas Berry has it, a human is 'that being in whom the universe comes to itself in a special mode of conscious reflection.' What are you looking into when you gaze into the face of another human being? There is every indication that you are seeing a hologram, a fragment that embodies and personifies the whole cosmos—and into whose hands at least this planet has cast its fate.
>
> And what are we humans, the observers, in this perspective? We come at the end of the cosmic meal, at the end of an enormously complex chain of conversions of noisy energy radiating to us in torrents and stretching back to the formation of galaxies out of the energy released by the Big Bang. Quite literally, we are the fallout of the stars, for without star factories converting helium out of hydrogen, there would be no oxygen, carbon, or iron; and without them there would be no amino acids or proteins for life; and without the radiation spilled over by the initial hydrogen-helium conversion, billions of stars would go dark. There would be no Sun, no day to nourish life.
>
> Like the stars, we too are dynamic energy systems, internally constituted by our relationships. We are open thermodynamic systems moving upstream and drifting toward

death; and thus, like the Sun and the Moon, we are disturbances in the field, vortices in turbulent nature. Like them we are constantly recycled, dissolving and reappearing. We grow our entire physical body as we do hair and nails. The tissue of our stomach renews itself weekly, the skin is shed monthly, and the liver regenerated every six weeks. Every moment a portion of the body's 10^{28} atoms is returning to the world outside, and ninety-eight percent of them are replaced annually.

Each time we breathe, we take in a quadrillion atoms breathed by the rest of humanity within the last two weeks and more than a million atoms breathed personally by each person on Earth. So much for the strictly bounded, separate individual."[5]

The Relationship Between The One and the Many

The physical body and the phenomenal ego are very much in flux. They make up the temporal persona that relates to the Transcendent. This temporal persona is the collection of all of those qualities of the individual by reason of its gender, race, nationality, religion, both inherited and programmed into the individual by family, school, religion, society, etc. This may be called the temporal image/phenomenal ego and is constantly changing as the individual establishes his/her place in society; and then further changes as the individual seeks her/his true self. These are the limitations the eternal spirit takes on upon entering the human experience.

---

[5] Fr. David S. Toolan, S. J., *Studies in the Spirituality of Jesuits*, The Seminar on Jesuit Spirituality (St. Louis: 1991) Father is quoting and summarizing from Larry Dossey's book, *Space, Time and Medicine* (Boulder: Shambala 1982).

There is THE ONE, the Mystery or Transcendence, the Source of all creation, yet totally immanent in the MANY of all of creation.

The relationship experienced by the many with the One is shaped and expressed within the images which derive from the perceived view of the Cosmos. The images are also formed by the social and political institutions of the many. These images may be very primitive or very sophisticated; they are nonetheless the groundwork or foundations for religions and cultures.

We call these images gods or even God and tend to forget the Mystery of which these images are no more than an attempt to say something of our experience with the Transcendent. We then tend to worship the images.

The Story of Snake

One day snake slithered inquiringly from its cave to find out from other creatures what was their image of God. The first creature is fox.

Snake: Fox, good day to you.
Fox: Good day to you also, Snake.
Snake: Fox, do you believe in God?
Fox: Why, of course.
Snake: What does God look like?
Fox: God is a great silver Fox, very cunning in her caring for the universe.
Snake: Thank you very much.
Fox: You are most welcome. Have a good day.

Snake continued on his journey and came to a great oak tree.
Snake: Good morning, O Majestic Oak tree.
Oak Tree: Good morning to you, snake.
Snake: Oak tree, do you believe in God?
Oak Tree: Why, of course.

Snake: What does God look like?
Oak Tree: God is a Great Beautiful Majestic Oak tree who gives shelter on its branches to the birds of the air and restful shade to all creatures who come to her.
Snake: Thank you very much.
Oak Tree: You are most welcome. Have a good day.

With Oak tree's permission Snake slithered up to one of its highest branches where it met owl.
Snake: Good morning, Owl.
Owl: Hoo— Hoo— Good morning to you, Snake.
Snake: Do you believe in God?
Owl: Why, of course.
Snake: What does God look like?
Owl: God is a great white Owl, who sits in silent wisdom to be shared with whomever will sit in silence with her.
Snake: Thank you very much.
Owl: You are most welcome.

Snake slithered towards its cave. Snake met human.
Snake: Good morning, Human.
Human: Good morning, Snake.
Snake: Do you believe in God?
Human: Of course.
Snake: What does God look like?
Human: Since we humans are made in the image and likeness of God, God must have an intellect and will, and be all knowing and all powerful, controlling the Universe.
Snake: you very much.
Human: You are most welcome.

Snake slithered back to its cave, called a meeting of all the other snakes and said, "The world is in great danger. No one knows that God is a Great Golden Snake. We must go out and convert all to the truth."

Images Formed by Perception of Cosmos

Human's perception of the Cosmos forms the basis for some of the images. For example Campbell notes the changes in our perception of the Universe which has evolved from the Sumero-Babylonian idea of a flat earth with a bowl on top, surrounded by water to the currently held belief that humanity is a recently evolved species on one of the smaller planets in one of the millions of galaxies.[6]

The traditional Judaeo-Christian image of the Cosmos and, therefore, of God was—and for many is still—precisely that of the Sumero-Babylonian image with a God outside of creation seated on a throne, determining all that is happening. Yet only in October of 1992 did a Vatican commission finally acknowledge that Galileo—who taught in the early 1600s and was imprisoned by church authorities for his 'radical' views—was not in error when he agreed with Copernicus (who died in 1543) that the Earth is not the center of the Universe.

Let's look at an image of God that would fit into what Campbell calls our present image of the Cosmos. Through the writings of Teilhard de Chardin, Brian Swimme, Thomas Berry and others, we are invited to an image of God as the Energy that draws all through evolution to the fullness of Cosmogenesis. This fits Campbell's image of exploding galaxies.

In reading Chardin's letters, our vision of the Cosmos, of The Christ and of the ultimate Reality-Mystery which we call God is opened. Therefore, our vision of the Spiritual Life is invited to expand beyond a rather narrow Judaeo-Christian vision to one that can simply be called Cosmic.

Thomas Merton gives us another image of Cosmogenesis:

---

[6] Cf. Joseph Campbell, *Inner Reaches of Outer Space* (New York: Harper & Row, 1988) p. 18.

> *Realization of the Supreme "Player" whose "play" (lila) is manifested in the million-formed inexhaustible richness of beings and events is what gives us the **key to the meaning of life. Once we live in awareness of the cosmic dance and move in time with the Dancer, our life attains its true dimensions** [emphasis mine]. It is at once more serious and less serious than the life of one who does not sense this inner cosmic dynamism.*[7]

This inner cosmic dynamism originates in the two-fold nature of human, in human's purpose in the evolutionary process of Planet Earth and of the Cosmos. It becomes very dynamic in the relationships of the phenomenal egos of each human, in the relationships of the humans to every other species on Planet Earth and in the Cosmos, and finally in the relationship of the many to the One. What a Cosmic Dance!

What is human and what is human's purpose? Earlier I quoted from Aldous Huxley's introduction to the *Bhagavad Gita:*

> Third: man possesses a double nature, a phenomenal ego and an eternal Self, which is the inner man, the spirit, the spark of divinity within the soul. It is possible for a man, if he so desires, to identify himself with the spirit and therefore with the Divine Ground, which is of the same or like nature with the spirit.[8]

Most humans tend to identify with the phenomenal ego. All their energy is focused on developing and preserving that dimension of themselves. It is called survival. **Anyone who loves his life loses it; anyone who hates his life in this world will keep it for the eternal life. (John 12:25)**. Only through crises are humans invited to become

---

[7] by Thomas Merton, from THE ASIAN JOURNALS OF THOMAS MERTON. Copyright © 1975 by The Trustees of the Merton Legacy Trust. Reprinted by permission of New Directions Publishing Corp. p.350

[8] Huxley, p. 13

deeply aware of the eternal Self which is the inner human, the spirit, the spark of divinity within the soul. Huxley indicates that this is the purpose of human's life:

> Fourth: man's life on earth has only one end and purpose: to identify with his eternal Self and so come to a unitive knowledge of the Divine Ground.[9]

Therein is human's part in the Cosmic Dance: the invitation to become aware of the Eternal Spirit/the One of which human's eternal Self is a spark. Becoming aware of this intuitively through many different passions, deaths, resurrections and ascensions, human is invited to become conscious of and to exult in the Cosmic Dance.

I do not understand what I am writing, but I do know that it is true.

Jesus is a Supreme Cosmic Dancer. He proclaims us to be one in the Father as He is in the Father and the Father in Him. He models for us what it means to be in this One. He invites us to join in this oneness. The oneness is there. We simply need become aware of what is and learn the major step of the Cosmic Dance—the Passover—which I will later describe.

> *I am the light of the world; anyone who follows me will not be walking in the dark; he will have the light of life.* John 8:12

Moving from the darkness which is within us to the light which is within us is a dimension of the Passover step of the Cosmic Dance. Moving from the darkness of temporal culture to the Eternal Light is another dimension of the Passover step of the Cosmic Dance. The invitation to the Cosmic Dance is both internal and external. Unless it takes place internally there is no real integration of the Dance and we keep stumbling all over ourselves and one another.

---

[9] Huxley, p. 13

PART II
Enter Angels and Other Cosmic Energies

> *"Now Paul was well aware that one section was made up of Sadducees and the other of Pharisees, so he called out to the Sanhedrin, 'Brothers, I am a Pharisee and the son of Pharisees. It is for our hope in the resurrection of the dead that I am on trial.' As soon as he said this a dispute broke out between the Pharisees and the Sadducees, and the assembly was split between the two parties. For the Sadducees say there is neither resurrection, nor angel, nor spirit, while the Pharisees accept all three. The shouting grew louder, and some of the scribes from the Pharisees' party stood up and protested strongly, 'We find nothing wrong with this man. Suppose a spirit has spoken to him, or an angel?'"*
>
> Acts 23:6-9.

Allow me to introduce you to my angel. Perhaps there are others but this one I know by name. This is how I came to know about her and get acquainted with her.

In early February of 1992 Dianne Markel, a friend, asked me to hypnotize her and help her become aware of her angels. I did so. As she became aware of two of her angels I asked her if she saw any around me. She was silent for a while then said, "Yes, I see a very beautiful woman's face. I don't see any body. She has very long blond hair. She is with you to help you in your writing and other creative endeavors." "Does she have a name?" I asked. There was a long pause. "The name Clarissa comes to me." I thanked her. We ended the session and I thought no more about Clarissa. I was working very hard and worrying a lot about a retreat I had coming up. I had prepared a lot of new material, and I was concerned about putting it together and about how it would be received. I was getting very tired. I had some pains in my chest, and because of a history of some slight heart trouble I went to see the doctor. He ordered a stress test. I passed the test with no problems.

A few nights later I had a dream:

> *It is late morning on a bright sunny day. The sense is that a convocation of students is being held outside the front of a library. The stage is the porch of the library. There are huge columns. I step up to a stately, well-dressed black woman who is in charge. I say, 'I need to get a file on Peter Faber.' She responds by waving me off and saying, 'We'll take care of that later.' Then I notice a high-backed, wooden, rather ornate chair a few feet in front of me. I can see only the back of the chair, but flowing on either side of the chair is long blonde hair. I walk toward the chair. The chair begins to move; it slides down some stairs onto the grass and then through a wooded trail into a lake. I am following the chair all the way down. When it goes into the lake, the occupant goes into the water. I go into the water. There is then a sense of playing with Clarissa.*

Upon reflection I realize that Peter Faber is an early Jesuit who is noted for his skill in directing others in the Spiritual Exercises of St. Ignatius of Loyola (or, giving a retreat). I also realize that his name means "work," like in prefabricated. I realize that I am invited by the feminine (the stately black woman) to put aside work and to play with Clarissa—she would help me. I did, and the retreat was very well received.

Some time later I was walking along Lake Pontchartrain near midnight. About 200 feet in front of me, 100 feet out over the lake, and about 50 feet high, I saw a very bright contained light about the size of a large grapefruit. It was moving very quickly toward the shore, leaving a short trail of light behind it. It appeared for about five seconds and then was gone. The next day as I was driving I was thinking that I would like to see Clarissa. What came to me was, "Who do you think you saw last night?"

After a year or so I began working on a manuscript which ultimately was submitted to my religious superiors in early September of 1994. For a number of good reasons the manuscript was rejected for publication. My angel, Clarissa, was aware that I had allowed some of my own personal negative feelings and misunderstandings to get into the manuscript. She decided to come live with me in the flesh of a little canine. She allowed me to get to know her and trust her and then she helped me to revise the manuscript. What you have now is the result of her help. Any confusion in what I have written is due to my misunderstanding of what Clarissa, in the form of a little canine, has been trying to convey to me.

Introducing Missy

On August 25, 1994 Clarissa, having decided to make herself more visible and tangible to me, enfleshed herself in a mixed breed canine body. She acted lost and homeless on the streets where Sr. Jo Ann Viviano, an incurable dog lover, would be passing by. Sure enough when Jo Ann saw this little dog, alone and homeless and seemingly in danger of being run over by cars, she opened her heart and the door to her car, whistled, and the dog who shall henceforth be called Missy jumped in.

Jo Ann and later Sr. Rosalie Ambler took Missy around the neighborhood to see if Missy would recognize any of the houses from which she might have come. They even put an ad in the paper. Of course, the results were negative. The Sisters realized they could not keep Missy in their quarters. They were looking for a home for Missy. And as Clarissa had planned, unbeknownst to any of us, I volunteered.

Missy is about seventeen pounds, stands about eighteen inches in height and is three feet long from the tip of her snout to the tip of her tail. She has brown sparkling eyes set in a pert, pretty little face. Her hair, from the top of her head down her back to the tip of her tail, is blonde. Her underhair is silky white from her chin to her fetlocks.

When she saunters out in front of me
Her light brown ears bounce jauntily.
Silky white hairs like pantaloons adorn.
Tail curving upwards—waves plumelike
An invitation to the Cosmic Dance.

Why Missy Is with Me

Missy is here to care for me. She is here to help me revise the manuscript. She takes me for walks and invites me to appreciate the beauty of the Cosmos, the embodiment of Spirit.

Sometimes I ask Missy to explain this and other mysteries to me. Most frequently she responds:

Larry, when will you learn? Enjoy the beauty! Be at one with the Mystery. Then you will know. Do you know why I made myself visible and tangible to you as a female canine?

Larry: Not really. I thought that if you were to make yourself visible at all you might appear something like Gabriella in Andrew Greeley's novel ANGEL FIRE.

Missy: Really, Larry, that isn't my style nor is it yours. I had a choice. Quite honestly I did not have the courage to choose to be a rational animal. Rationality is indeed a blessing but it is also a curse. It is a curse because it is so intriguing that rational animals individually and collectively frequently think they can analyze, understand and then control the whole of Cosmogenesis. I chose as an intuitive angel to be an instinctive, sensate non-rational animal. What I intuit in the Universe I communicate directly to your intuition, thus by-passing as much as possible all the labyrinthine ways of the rational intellect.

Larry: Now, Missy, you know as well as I that the rational intellect of humans is what sets them above the non-rational animal kingdom.

Missy: Why, of course, that is what you humans say. Just as you humans say that you, and by implication only you, are made in the image and likeness of God.

Larry: That is what we have been taught.

Missy: Don't you think the whole of Cosmogenesis images God Who is the Source of Cosmogenesis?

Larry: Whew! I guess so.

Missy: That is why I am here. I want to free you from your anthropocentric teachings. I want to invite you to experience the wonder of yourself as an eternal spirit courageously bringing light, compassion and love into the darkness of the evolutionary process of the rational animal. It is important for you and all humans to know that the rational animal simply does not realize that it is only one of thousands of species on Planet Earth. Not realizing this human has become so arrogant as to think it has dominion over the Earth and even that it is the center of the Universe. Furthermore human is so irrationally rational about survival that human is destroying Planet Earth, the very source of human's survival.

Larry: You know all that?

Missy: It is so absolutely clear to all the angels, to all in the Cosmos, that the rational human is destroying itself by its irrational placing of itself at the apex and center of Planet Earth and, indeed, of the Universe. And, Larry, please hear me.....*We angels and all cosmic energies stand in awe as we witness you eternal spirits, the most courageous in the Universe, choosing to participate in the redemptive process of the human species by bringing light, compassion and love into such darkness and greed rooted in the fallacious need to survive.*[1]

---

[1] cf. Bartholomew. *I Come as a Brother.* (Taos, New Mexico: The High Mesa Foundation, 1986) p. 175.

Larry: Thank you, Missy, that is very encouraging for me and I am sure for all humans who may be able to hear that deeply within themselves. It reminds me of the saying of Jesus, "Let him who has ears to hear, hear." By the way, Missy, why do you choose to share all of this with me?

Missy: Well, Larry, it's like this. You are one of the least academically trained old priests we could find. And you know that you slept throughout the course on Logic. So you are not too concerned about analyzing or proving my existence or anything I share with you. Speaking of Jesus... Larry, do you understand the story of Jesus the Christ and the purpose of it?

Larry: The story of Jesus the Christ?

Missy: Yes.

Larry: (I did not want to get into this. It seemed to be too much. So I responded.) No. I consider that a mystery.

Missy: (Missy would not accept this.) My good man.........You are in your seventy-fifth year and in your forty-fifth year as a priest and that is all you can say?

Larry: Okay, the way that I understand Jesus the Christ is that His purpose is to free each one of us to become who we are.

Missy: That is exactly right...to find the Christness in your being—to understand that all humans must get to a place in which they celebrate the wonder of themselves. Christ gave to human the image of what human must become. And that was the purpose of His life. His purpose is not to be worshipped, but to teach human that within human there is the temporal persona or ego and there is divinity, or the eternal spirit, that is one in the One. Each individual is invited during the course of his/her life to bring the persona into harmony with her/his eternal spirit.

Larry: What I am beginning to pick up is something I have thought; namely, that what is important is being present to mystery, and letting go of the concepts.

Missy: That is truth!

Larry: So that knowledge is not conceptualized, but is union with mystery. Is that it?

Missy: Absolutely! It is the same.

Larry: So the concepts get in the way of the mystery. Is that it?

Missy: You lose perspective of what you're seeking to find. (I'm laughing.) Human must keep it simple. When human starts confusing the issues then human has lost human's place.

Larry: How does human confuse the issues?

Missy: By trying to understand everything with the implication that once the mystery is understood then it can be lived. Human is invited to trust that the teachings which are needed for the present moment are within. Indeed they are within the cellular wisdom developed over the millenia. But when human forgets that humans are part of the One in the Cosmic Dance and live out of their own separatenesses, then humans begin to fear and worry, lose trust in themselves and in the Universe and live life, as Merton says, "as beasts of burden."

Larry: Thank you, Missy.

Missy: I have something to add. In this life simplicity is the key that allows all to feel Oneness. It is surrender to mystery which is acceptance, which is love.

And here our dialogue ended.

Being a good Pharisee I firmly believe that there are the angels and other cosmic consciousnesses, energies, all about us, and for that matter in us, and neither in us nor outside us. In fact, we humans may be only a small physical expression of consciousnesses in the Cosmos. I also believe, but cannot prove to any doubter's satisfaction, that communication takes place intuitively between we incarnated cosmic consciousnesses and those that are not incarnated or maybe incarnated in non-rational animals. All of this is expressed imaginatively and in the expression realized more fully. Garrett Green in his work *Imagining God* proposes the imagination as the primary arena in which God works and plays to reveal God's self. Perhaps that is why St. Ignatius, in his Spiritual Exercises, always invited the exercitant to use the imagination.

PART III
Missy Speaks on Religion

The Purpose of Religion

Larry: Missy, please speak to me about religion.

Missy: Religion is the most important dimension of human's existence. Religion has as its purpose preserving the stories of the experiences of the human with the Transcendent. It passes these stories to future generations so they in turn may identify with their ancestors' experiences, be encouraged by them and so be empowered with trust in the Transcendent to move into the unknown—the new—the not yet. Without these ancestral stories individuals would be born into a vacuum. It would be like not knowing who they are or where they came from.

Larry: May I assume that religion is something of a stabilizing influence in the continuing evolutionary process of the human species?

Missy: Yes, religion gives individuals an identity in their relationship with their ancestors and their God. Individuals are invited and empowered to live their lives with moral values appropriate to their culture and, in many instances with compassion and love for other humans. All of the arts are enobled as they are used to express these relationships. In many traditions, especially in the West, religion has spawned and developed the revered intellectual tradition of Theology and Philosophy as its handmaidens. Religion is indeed a very integral and important dimension of the human experience.

Larry: Then why is it that so many people, good people, have difficulty with religion?

Missy: Larry, the first thing to keep in mind is that religion is made for human and not human for religion. This is expressed very well in the story given in the Gospel according to Mark, "One Sabbath day he happened to be taking a walk through the cornfields, and his disciples began to pick ears of corn as they went along. And the Pharisees said to him, 'Look, why are they doing something on the Sabbath day that is forbidden?'And he replied, 'Did you never read what David did in his time of need when he and his followers were hungry — how he went into the house of God when Abiathar was high priest, and ate the loaves of offering which only the priests are allowed to eat, and how he also gave some to the men with him?' And he said to them, 'The sabbath was made for man not man for the sabbath; so the son of Man is master even of the sabbath.'" (Mark 2:23-28)

Larry: Come on, Missy, are you trying to say that Jesus was against religion?

Missy: Of course not. As he said, "I have come not to destroy the Law but to bring it to its fulfillment." (Matt. 5:17). Later Paul wrote in his letter to the Ephesians, "For he is the peace between us, and has made the two into one and broken down the barrier which used to keep them apart, actually destroying in his own person the hostility caused by the Law." (Ephesians 2:14). This Law is religion. The remainder of that chapter speaks of the unity of all in Christ. This is the Cosmic Spirit—the One in which humans and all creatures—even non-rational animals, canines like myself—are the many. Did Jesus as the incarnation of the Cosmic Spirit come to call all creatures out of their separatenesses and invite all, especially humans, to be aware of their essential, eternal unity in the One? Yes.

Larry: I am under the impression that you are saying that religions tend to separate humans from one another.

Missy: Yes, of course, all you have to do is to look at the many religious wars throughout history.

Larry: But, Missy, aren't religions supposed to invite humans to worship God, Who loves all as His children?

Misunderstandings Can Cause Wars

Missy: Sure, that is true. But remember that each religion has its own human expression of how the ancestors experienced God or gods. The Creed, Code and Cult—Doctrines, Laws and Rituals based on these experiences become very sacred to the people of each religion. Without realizing it the religion tends to take the place of God. And when religions—the expressions of the experiences with the Transcendent—differ they tend to divide, cause tensions and conflicts—even **wars.**

Larry: We humans really seem to want to hold on to what we have—our property, our mindset, our status quo in any dimension of life.

Missy: Yes, Larry, its based on the fallacious need to survive by understanding and controlling. All of those dimensions of humans' lives tend to become like household gods. You remember the story in Exodus, the Hebrews had to discard their household gods in the desert in order to follow the pillar of fire by night and the cloud by day. So must humans' household gods be discarded as human moves through the evolutionary process of the species, of the planet, of the universe.

Larry: Are you saying that religion as a whole and/or different aspects of religion can be compared to the household gods of the Hebrews?

Missy. Yes. For the movement of Cosmogenesis is always in the **not yet** even though it may take centuries in time and space to become aware of the new.

Larry: But we are taught to revere religion—the creed, code, and cult—as though it were given to us by God and engraved in stone.

Missy: Yes. That is true. That also is rooted in the human desire for security in human's compulsion to understand and control in order to survive. Actually the story of the Exodus and in fact the whole of the Judaeo-Christian Scriptures are an invitation to **trust** the Transcendent

God leading humans in their individual and collective passovers.

Larry: So what about reverence?

Missy: Reverence is shown in accepting the invitation to **trust.** As humans revere and are grateful to their parents, grandparents and all who have nutured them, so are they invited to revere and be grateful for their religious traditions which have nourished them.

Larry: So the hymn *Give Me That Ol' Time Religion* has merit?

Missy: No, Larry, that is not the same thing. To revere it does not mean to hold on to it. It means to be grateful for the nourishment and support and then to go on to the next step in the Cosmic Dance. Perhaps it is well to remember the incident recorded in Mark's gospel. "His mother and brothers arrived and, standing outside, sent in a message asking for him. A crowd was sitting round him at the time the message was passed to him, 'Your mother and brothers and sisters are outside asking for you.' He replied, 'Who are my mother and my brothers?' And looking round at those sitting in a circle about him, he said, 'Here are my mother and my brothers. Anyone who does the will of God, that person is my brother, and sister and mother.'" (Mark 3:31-35).

Larry: I'm afraid you lost me.

Missy: What that means is that those who were doing the will of God are the ones who nourished Jesus.

Invitation to Changing Images

Now let's make a big jump in your thinking. As you humans approach the twenty-first century **to do the will of God** may be expressed in less anthropomorphic terms such as **to be in harmony with the Energy Source of Cosmogenesis.** This calls for a paradigmatic shift in human's imaging the Transcendent. Chardin wrote of God as the Love Energy of Cosmogenesis.

Larry: Missy, are you telling me that you know about Teilhard de Chardin and his writings?

Missy: Larry, all the other angels and I were jumping with joy—to use a human metaphor—when Chardin was expressing his insights into the evolutionary process of Planet Earth and even of the Universe. We also rejoiced when Thomas Aquinas wrote in his *Contra Gentiles* that all of nature is the primary revelation of the Divine. To help him was one of my assignments. One of my greatest experiences with Tom was when he was near the time of leaving his body. I danced his spirit through the Milky Way and then through a few other galaxies. When his spirit was back in his body he was both laughing and crying. Speaking of all he had written he said, "Missy, *omnia sicut palea,*" or, it is all like chaff.

Larry: Let's go back to the writings of Chardin about Cosmogenesis and imaging God as the Energy Source of Cosmogenesis. Are you inviting me and other humans who care to listen into a great big paradigmatic shift in our way of thinking of God and Religion?

Missy: Yes. Remember God remains the incomprehensible Transcendent Mystery as always. What is changing is the way in which you humans are invited to image God. I know you slept through most of the course in logic but you may remember the distinction between **id quod** and **modus quo**. The **id quod** is the **that which.** The **id quod** in our discussion is the Incomprehensible Mystery of the Transcendent and Human's experience of this Mystery. The **modus quo** is the **manner in which** that experience is experienced and then expressed, namely, the Creed, Code and Cult. These three constitute religion.

Larry: So we humans are invited to allow the **modus quo** to continually change with the evolutionary process of the species while holding on to and **trusting** the Incomprehensible Mystery—the **id quod.**

Missy: That is correct. And there are times when the changes into which you are invited are more noticeable.

Larry: We humans don't like to do that.

Missy: That is true. From my vantage point as an angel intuitively perceiving the Universe, you humans are like the disciples of Jesus. The disciples marvelled at the beauty of the Temple. And Jesus said, "You see all these? I tell you solemnly, not a single stone will be left on another. Everything will be destroyed." (Matthew 24:2). The same can be said of any religion. Its houses of worship may all be destroyed; its Creed, Code and Cult may all cease. What remains is human in human's evolutionary process, human's relationship to all the other species on planet Earth and indeed to the Universe and the immanent presence of the Transcendent Mystery—the Energy Source of Cosmogenesis. As snake sheds its skin and lives on, so human is continually invited to shed the time-space constructs of religion and move into the new, the not yet, with **trust.**

Why Such Resistance to Change

Larry: OK Miss, can you tell me now exactly why it is that we humans are resistant to the on-going changes in religion that are demanded by Cosmogenesis?

Missy: (She is laughing) Larry, you didn't even want to change the manuscript—to rewrite the expressions of your own ideas! (She is referring to the fact that the Advisors to my religious superior suggested changes in the first writing of the manuscript. When I was invited to change it I wanted to hold on to some of the expressions simply because they were mine and had become sacred to me.)

Larry: OK OK Now please tell me more.

Missy: The beloved Rabbi Abraham Joshua Heschel once wrote something to the effect that insights once conceptualized tend to fossilize. And as St. Stephen said to the members of the Sanhedrin (referring to the worship of the golden calf), "They were perfectly happy with something they had made for themselves." (Acts 7:41) And so, my dear Larry, it frequently happens that much if not all of the energy of human goes into preserving and quibbling over the precise meanings of the expressions of what has been. They like to celebrate what has been. They find such security in these exercises that their whole beings remain closed to the invitation to move into the unknown—the new—the not yet. Then the purpose of religion as a dynamic, life empowering proclamation— that God has been compassionately present to them from the beginning, is compassionately present to them now and will be compassionately present to them in the future as they go through their various passovers individually and collectively—is frustrated. Humans simply become more concerned with the Creed, Code, and Cult which tell them what has been, and so are closed to the invitation to the next passover step of the Cosmic Dance. They learn how not to hear what they should be listening to.

Larry: My dear Missy, do you have any suggestions for us humans?

Missy: Yes! Wake up! Become aware of what you have done to the gift of religion. Instead of using it as a support system in the journey you tend to worship **religion** rather than worshipping God. Let's just take a look at how religions develop, and I'm going to use the Roman Catholic Church as an example. You grew up in that religion. It has served you and millions of others very well over the centuries.

The development of Religions may have gone something like this:

1. The experience of the Transcendent by the human
2. The imaging of the experience
3. The conceptualizing of the image
4. The wording of the concept
5. The story of the experience
6. The discussion of the meaning of the story
7. A **Creed** to which all can agree
(this is a lowest common denominator of the meaning)
8. A **Code:** the combination of cultural customs influenced by the Creed
(this may gradually include a body of legislation)
9. A **Cult:** a manner of worship appropriate to the Creed, Code and Culture of the people
10. An Ecumenical Council to determine what the Creed means
11. Theological discussions to determine what the documents of the Ecumenical Councils mean
12. An adult catechism to bring the teachings to the laity
13. Finally, a children's catechism with which most have been raised, and by which many continue to live as they learned it as children

Larry: Thanks, Missy, for that outline. I and thousands of others in the United States learned the teachings of the Church through the Baltimore Catechism which dates back to April 6, 1885.

Missy. You did some research on that didn't you?

Larry: It was very easy, Missy. I found it on the inside of the front cover of a 1933 edition of the Catechism once used by my brother, Kenneth. I discovered the book in the attic of my parents' house when I cleaned it out a few years ago. You must know, Missy, that every Catholic girl and boy had to memorize the smaller Catechism before they made their First Communion, and then a larger Catechism before they could be confirmed and make what was called their Solemn Communion. We were well taught. I am told, though I have no proof of this, that this was true for other countries throughout the world wherever the Catholic Church thrived.

Missy: Yes, that is true. This developed generations of Catholics with a firm grasp of the doctrines of the Catholic Church in Catechetical form. Since there was little or no understanding of symbolism, it was all taken as literal truth.

Larry: Why are we discussing this? Where is the problem?

Missy: The problem is that in trusting the literalness of the catechism answers, individuals tended to think that there is no mystery—that they know what the mystery is all about because they have the answers. To put it bluntly, Larry, as youngsters you were accustomed to being catechised and told what to do and how to think. In school you were programmed to learn by conceptualizing, analyzing, and proving.

Larry: Wasn't that a necessary structure for us as we were growing?

Missy: By all means. But little value was placed on intuition and a feeling of awe before the mystery of Transcendence revealing, manifesting, in the phenomena of the universe. One way of interpreting the story of the Fall is that humans lost their sense of awe of the mystery of the Transcendent when they ate of the Tree of Knowledge.

You must understand, Larry, intuitive knowledge is what Jesus is speaking about when He says that one can not enter the kingdom of God unless one becomes as a little child—a child who has not yet been taught the names of anything, but simply marvels and dances in glee with all of creation. Most humans don't remember the state of being in a sense of awe. Early on you humans were taught to "know" so that you could survive in your time-space experience.

> *At this time the disciples came to Jesus and said, 'Who is the greatest in the kingdom of heaven?' So he called a little child to him and set the child in front of them. Then he said, 'I tell you solemnly, unless you change and become like little children you will never enter the kingdom of heaven. And so, the one who makes himself as little as this little child is the greatest in the kingdom of heaven.'* Matthew 18:1-4

> *At that time Jesus exclaimed, 'I bless you, Father, Lord of heaven and of earth, for hiding these things from the learned and the clever and revealing them to mere children. Yes, Father, for that is what it pleased you to do.'* Matthew 11:25-26

Larry: Missy, I have a story for you.

Missy: Good. I like stories.

Larry: The following was told to me as a true story.

> A young couple had a little boy about four years of age. The couple then had another little baby. One day when the baby was about three months old and lying in its crib in the nursery the little four-year-old asked his parents if he could speak to Baby. The parents said, "Of course, let's go in and talk to Baby now." The four-year-old said "No, I want to talk to Baby alone." The parents said, "Okay, you go in while we stand here at the door." The four-year-old said, "No, I want the door closed." The parents said, "Okay, after awhile." They set up a monitor so they could hear what was going on, then they told the boy he could go in. Making sure the door was closed so that his parents could not hear, the boy went over to the crib and said to the baby, "Tell me what God looks like. I'm beginning to forget."

Missy: I like that story. Remember it is quite possible that the untaught child has an intuitive sense of the Transcendent, the Divine Ground, and the Mystery, but gradually loses it as the eternal Self is taught more fully the trappings of time and space. As the temporal persona develops there is less awareness of the eternal Self.

Larry: May I assume that union of the human with the Transcendent takes place through an intuitive experience? Whatever images, concepts and words we may use to describe the experience to ourselves and others greatly limit the experience. We seem caught in the fallacy that if we can't articulate the experience in some manner, then it is not valid. As A.A. Milne's "Winnie-the Pooh" and "Piglet" agree, "Rabbit" is clever and has a Brain, but that is why Rabbit doesn't understand. The experience of Transcendence in its purity, in its quintessential thusness is not communicable. Whatever images, words or movements—such as dance, music or drumming—we may use to help us express our experience of the Mystery are certainly valid but limiting; they simply fall short of the experience. How is that Missy?

Missy: Considering the limitations of language and your own limitations you are doing rather well. And I might add, what you have said is true of the *Bible,* the *Koran,* the *Tao te Ching,* the *Bhagavad Gita,* and any other Sacred Scriptures of the various religions of the planet. No written word exhausts the Transcendent Mystery. Joseph Campbell says that even the *Kena Upanishad,* written in the 7th Century, B.C. says very clearly that the Transcendent is that which words and thoughts do not reach.[2]

Larry: Thank you, Missy. And now if you don't mind I'm going to do a little monologue.

Missy: Be my guest.

Larry: We cannot know the Transcendent intellectually or conceptually. We can only be united with it in the daily and nightly rhythms of the Cosmic Dance; being in harmony with the Eternal Dancer Who is also the Choreog-

---

[2] Phil Cousineau, ed. *The Hero's Journey: Joseph Campbell on His Life and Work* (New York: Harper & Row, 1990) p. 47

rapher, without asking why—simply allowing oneself to be led into the next step of the dance.

The Lost Pearl

The Yellow Emperor went wandering
To the north of the Red Water
To the Kwan Lun mountain. He looked around
Over the edge of the world. On the way home
He lost his night-colored pearl
He sent out Science to seek his pearl, and got nothing.
He sent Analysis to look for his pearl, and got nothing.

He sent out Logic to seek his pearl, and got nothing.
Then he asked Nothingness,
and Nothingness had it!
The Yellow Emperor said:
'Strange, indeed: Nothingness
Who was not sent
Who did not work to find it
Had the night-colored pearl!'[3]

To use words for the Transcendent Mystery, the Source of the Cosmos, is at the very least to babble but more easily borders on blasphemy. And yet what are we humans to do? We risk using metaphors because when we do we then have a tendency to turn them into prosaic facts. Then, like children with building blocks, we construct various systems; we compare our systems and argue about the truth or falsity of each. Lo and behold, we have created our own gods, our own religions, each with its own Creed, Code and Cult. **We have forgotten the experience of the Transcendent Mystery.** Having diversified ourselves we then divide ourselves against

---

[3] by Chuang Tzu, translated by Thomas Merton, from THE WAY OF CHUANG TZU. p. 74. Copyright © 1965 by The Abbey of Gethesemani. Reprinted by permission of New Directions Publishing Corp.

one another; we build cultures around our religions and go to **war**. And if we are not at war with other religions and cultures we expend a lot of energy analyzing our metaphorical concepts as though they are facts. They become fossilized and lose their life because they are no longer pointing to the Transcendent Mystery but to themselves.

Missy: My dear Larry, I think you are beginning to learn.

PART IV
Death is an Illusion

At that time Jesus exclaimed, 'I bless you, Father, Lord of heaven and of earth, for hiding these things from the learned and the clever and revealing them to mere children. Yes, Father, for that is what it pleased you to do.' Matthew 11:25-26

I asked a little child, "What happens when a seed is planted?"
The little child responded, "It dies."
I asked the litle child, "If it dies, how can it grow?"
The little child responded, "It doesn't die dead, it dies live."

For we know that when the tent we live in on earth is folded up, there is a house built by God for us, an everlasting home not made by human hands, in the heavens.

We are always full of confidence, then, when we remember that to live in the body means to be exiled from the Lord, going as we do by faith and not by sight—we are full of confidence, I say, and actually want to be exiled from the body and make our home with the Lord. Whether we are living in the body or exiled from it we are intent on pleasing him. 2 Cor:5:1; 6-8

In the first Preface of the Masses for the Dead in the Roman Sacramentary may be found these words:

In him, who rose from the dead, our hope of resurrection dawned. The sadness of death gives way to the bright promise of immortality.

Lord, for your faithful people **life is changed, not ended** [emphasis mine]. When the body of our earthly dwelling lies in death we gain an everlasting dwelling place in heaven.

As a matter of fact, the whole of our Christian belief centers around the fact that the Soul is eternal and that Death is an Illusion.

Life is changed, not ended. The soul is no longer a prisoner in this corruptible body—wherein it experiences primarily the separateness of the many. Freed from this corruptible body it experiences primarily unity in the One, wherein there is neither male nor female, neither Jew nor Greek, neither slave nor free. cf. Galatians 3:27; Mark 12:25

For most humans the persona consciousness is not aware that death is an illusion. The persona consciousness is aware of its gender, its race, its nationality, its religion, its social and economic status, its desires, its goals, but most of all its **need** to survive. Therefore it focuses its energy and attention on those identities which most assure its survival. St. Paul would call this dimension of himself his unspiritual self, as opposed to his inmost self or true self. This is darkness, missing the mark, hemertia—(the Greek word for sin). It is this sin from which we need salvation. Let's play with this Sin/Darkness in Chapter V.

PART V

I Am
the Light
of the World

I am the light of the world;
anyone who follows me will not be walking in the dark;
he will have the light of life.
John 8:12

    In this section I wish to play with the mysteries of sin, sins, sacrifice, salvation by atonement, and salvation by enlightenment. The reason for doing this is that the Spiritual Exercises for Compassionate Energies participating in the Evolutionary Process of the Human Species follows in the next section, and the first exercises are on sin. I wish to make it abundantly clear that I am putting the emphasis on sin/darkness and Salvation by Christ the Light while acknowledging the reality of personal sins.

Images of the Transcendent

    Earlier on I mentioned that for the purpose of sharing our experiences of the Transcendent we necessarily use images of a particular culture expressed in concepts in a particular language. These images arise in some manner out of our social, political, and economic culture.
    I suggest four images for consideration: the first is that of the Tribal Chieftain or King. He is the sole Ruler. His people depend on him for their well-being. He will do what he needs to do to insure for them a reasonably good life and retain his power over them. He will make demands on them and he will insist that his will, the royal decrees, be observed. If they are not observed the offender is punished.

If the offender persists in his/her evil ways the offender may be banished from the Tribe or Kingdom. Because something of a personal relationship has been established between the Chieftain and his subjects, the Chieftain or the King is personally offended when any one of his subjects goes against his will—violates the law.

The second image is drawn from the gospels. One is given in Luke:15—the wonderful story of the Prodigal/Passionately loving Father. His younger son has squandered his share of the inheritance on a life of debauchery. When he returns to his Father, the Father does not ask him what he has done or why he has done it. The Father accepts him back unconditionally. And in the fifth chapter of Matthew's gospel Jesus says:

> *But I say this to you: Love your enemies and pray for those who persecute you, in this way you will be children of your Father in heaven, for he causes his sun to rise on bad men as well as good, and his rain to fall on honest and dishonest men alike....You must therefore set no bounds to your love as your Heavenly Father sets none to His. Jerusalem Bible, 1985*

> *Be compassionate as you Father is compassionate. Do not judge and you will not be judged yourselves; Do not condemn, and you will not be condemned yourselves. Luke 6:36&37.*

Again, there is a person-to-person relationship but now it is between parent and child. The parent loves the child unconditionally. The parent is not offended. The parent is too passionately loving to be offended by children who miss the mark.

The third image is given to me by a friend, Barbara Erichson. Barbara has in the recent past taught pre-K autistic children. These children may have scratched her, pinched her, even bitten her, and carried on in all sorts of ways that are detrimental to her and to her work. She was not offended. She knew that the children were autistic, profoundly handicapped, caught up in their own little worlds with their needs for structure, the desire to communicate and the inability to do so. With this disability came frustration, anxiety, fear, anger, etc. Barbara images God as a Pre-K Teacher and all of us humans as autistic, and profoundly handicapped.

On the Cosmic Scale we are. We live in our own little worlds fashioned for each of us by our DNA as well as the programming experienced by our particular ethnic cultures. The result is a difficulty in knowing the uniqueness of ourselves which we somehow experience. Consequently we have tremendous difficulties communicating with all around us. Out of sheer frustration, anxiety, fear and anger, many of us end up acting in many inappropriate ways which we have been taught offend God. I suggest that we do not **offend** God; we simply act inappropriately, going against the right order of things, hurting ourselves and others.

The fourth image is that of the One and the Many dancing the Cosmic Dance as described in Chapter I. The One is the Cosmic Dancer choreographing and dancing the cosmic dance of which each and all of us are ephemeral epiphanies. As Shakespeare so eloquently says,

Out, out, brief candle!
Life's but a walking shadow, a poor player,
That struts and frets his hour upon the stage,
And then is heard no more.

Our separateness and diversity by which we divide ourselves one against the other are ephemeral. Yet we identify with our separateness and think our ephemeralness is the totality of our individual existences. **This identification is our Sin/Darkness.** Our sins (plural) are all those thoughts, words and actions which emphasize our separateness and desire to survive in our ephemeralness—the temporal persona. This puts us out of harmony with the Cosmic Dancer and with the choreographed Cosmic Dance. We stumble all over ourselves and one another.

In this image there is no personal relationship with the Transcendent—the Cosmic Dancer, because there is no persona unless we project a persona onto the Transcendent, as we do in the first three mentioned above. No persona of the Transcendent is offended. Individually we get hurt because we are not in step with the Cosmic Dance. We hardly disturb the Cosmic Dance which is trillions of times larger than Planet Earth, so how much larger than each of us in our separateness.

Cosmic Irreversible Transitions and Transformations
*

Passovers

The image of the Cosmic Dance is simply another way of expressing the story of the Universe—Cosmogenesis—the continual bursting forth of the new. In this reality there are many microcosmic and macrocosmic irreversible transitions and transformations which have taken and are taking place. All of them require a dying to what is, that the new may live. Scientists tell us that some four and a half billion years ago there was a supernova which they called Tiamet. When it exploded it died to itself and gave life to our galaxy—the Milky Way—of which Planet Earth and each of us individually is a part.

Something of the same happens microcosmically. One day I asked a little boy what happens to a seed when it is planted. He said, "It dies." I asked. "If it dies how can anything come out of it?" He looked at me as though I knew nothing and answered, "It don't die dead. It dies live!" This sums up the story of the Universe and introduces us humans into the need to trust the Universe of which we are psychic-spiritual as well as physical-material dimensions.

On Planet Earth in the Judaeo-Christian tradition these irreversible transitions and transformations may be called Passovers. For many it is the most difficult and frightening of movements in the Cosmic Dance. It is the movement from the known to the unknown, from the familiar to the unfamiliar, but also from slavery to freedom. In the Judaeo-Christian tradition there is the Passover of a People—the Hebrews are led by Moses from Egypt into the Promised Land. This was a very difficult irreversible transition but also a transformation of tribes into a dominant people.

In Jesus of Nazareth there is the Passover of an individual. For Jesus there was the movement from the sin/darkness within himself to an awareness of his oneness with the Father. This is indicated in the following passages.

> "For our sakes God made him who did not know sin to be sin, so that in him we might become the very holiness of God." 2 Cor. 5:21.

> "In your minds you must be the same as Christ Jesus;
> His state was divine
> yet he did not cling
> to his equality with God
> but emptied himself
> to assume the condition of a slave
> and became as men are."
>   Philippians, 2:5-7.

When Jesus comes to an awareness that he and all humans are children of God he proclaims this wherever he goes. **He is the Light.** John 8:12. This proclamation brings him into conflict with the religious-political powers of his people. **This is the Darkness.** John 3:19. This struggle is climaxed in his crucifixion. He rises from the dead and ascends to his Father. This is his passover. He enters into it and goes through it with the courage, strength and trust that he is indeed one with the Father, that his spirit is eternal. This is another way of saying that he is one of the many in the One.

Jesus of Nazareth merges into the Cosmic Dance as the superb Cosmic Dancer. He is for many the Way, the Truth and the Life. He invites us to become aware that we, though many, are one in the One as He is one in the One and the One is in Him and in us. To experience this is a movement from our separateness or Sin/Darkness which seems to be light to the Light which seems to be darkness. Finally, for many it is the movement from Religion to Faith.

> *As for the Law, I was a Pharisee; as for working for religion, I was a persecutor of the Church; as far as the Law can make you perfect, I was faultless. But because of Christ, I have come to consider all these advantages that I had as disadvantages. Not only that, but I believe nothing can happen that will outweigh the supreme advantage of knowing Christ Jesus my Lord. For him I have accepted the loss of everything and look on everything as so much rubbish if only I can have Christ and be given a place in Him. I am no longer trying for perfection by my own efforts, the perfection that comes from the Law, but I want only the perfection that comes through faith in Christ, and is from God and is based on faith.* Philippians 3:6-9

This is an invitation to the dance, to experience a Passover, an irreversible transition, an irreversible transformation. The ultimate, of course, is to go through the illusion of death. In this most difficult and important of movements in the Cosmic Dance, Jesus of Nazareth is indeed Son of God modelling for us what it means to be children of God.

This Passover which is played out externally has profound meaning for those engaged in the spiritual journey. This is the journey of the persona identified with and engaged in the struggle for survival in the external world. The journey is a gradual awareness of its soul, its cosmic spirit, which is quite beyond conceptualization and yet is intuitively known to be its quintessential thusness.

This is the Passover experience. With this awareness the soul is invited to die to its identification with its ephemeral epiphany, to rise and to ascend to its true self.

These are musings based on our ancient symbols, traditional spiritual writers and forty-five years of priesting. Intuitively I know they manifest reality.

Jesus is the Image of the Invisible Transcendent compassionately present to enlighten us as the Choreographer invites us to go though our individual passovers, the most difficult and frightening of movements of the Cosmic Dance. He is also the archetype of the compassionate presence, courage, strength and trust within each of us that empowers us to live passionately as we go through these passovers; enjoying, struggling, suffering, dying, rising and ascending to our true selves.

Images Again

The first image of the tribal chieftain is used frequently in the Old Testament and is drawn from the social, political and economic experience of the people of that time. They were tribes trying to survive and they experienced the Transcendent with them; they imaged the Transcendent as something of a tribal chieftain.

The second is the image that Jesus uses and is drawn from the human family in which the Father of the family has all the power and is unconditionally loving; he just doesn't know the good from the bad or the honest from the dishonest. Those are terms that come from the acculturation, not from the family. The family is a place of refuge and security in the midst of the social, political and economic struggles of living.

The third is the image of the Transcendent that cannot be offended, but is simply compassionately present to us as we struggle in our autism or oughtism—experiences of being conditioned and programmed by our social, religious, political and economic cultures.

The fourth image of the Cosmic Dancer is the same as the third in its consequences that it can not be offended.

As far as I can remember I never heard or read of the image of the tribal chieftain used for the Transcendent except in Joseph Campbell's *The Inner Reaches of Outer Space.* I use it because it summarizes for me and others the sin/darkness in which many of us have lived. This is a result of taking catechetical teachings literally and accepting as univocal statements what were meant to be analogous statements by our teachers. The sin/darkness is missing the mark, being confused and having very inadequate concepts of God and human and human's relationship to God and to one another. This is no one's fault. It is simply part of human's desire to know and categorize the mysteries of human and God and all of the Universe.

The first image of the Transcendent as a tribal chieftain calls for obedience to the Chief. Going against the Chief's mandates requires punishment and, for the reprobate, banishment from the tribe. When this image is projected onto the Transcendent by us humans we end up with the teachings with which most Catholics grew up in the last millennium.

Sins

My perception of what I was taught, and it seems to be the perception of all who were raised with the *Baltimore Catechism,* is that sin is any willful thought, word, deed or omission contrary to the law of God and is an offense against God, as though God is hurt and takes the offense personally. Since God is infinite, and human is finite, human cannot satisfy the infinite justice of God or satisfy the infinite dignity of the person of God. Therefore, the second person of the Blessed Trinity became human and, being both God and human, could and did satisfy the infinite justice and the offended dignity of God by the bloody sacrifice of his death on the cross. This is called a propitiatory sacrifice.

One of the consequences of this teaching is that we learned that each of us, by our sins, has made Jesus suffer because He had to satisfy God the Father for us. Imagine or remember the guilt that was laid on us as children, and even as adults, when it was preached to us that we caused the bloody sweat in the garden, the scourging, the crowning with thorns, the way of the cross and the pain of the crucifixion. I preached this in many retreats and I was right in line with the other preachers.

Along with this agony we were taught to accept our sufferings and unite them to the sufferings of Jesus to atone for the sins of the world. This creates a "victim spirituality" which, in turn, creates an unacknowledged image of a God Who somehow needs our suffering, our atonement, to balance the offenses and insults He experiences by the sins of humanity.

Imaging God as something of a Tribal Chieftain who can be offended and somehow or other needs to be appeased by a propitiatory sacrifice engenders fear and guilt and, I suspect, a tremendous dose of unacknowledged resentment from which springs anger and rebelliousness. When these feelings are not acknowledged, neurotic behavior results. In my forty-five years of priesting I have witnessed hundreds of people in great pain and suffering because of their fear and anxiety and irrational guilt, all of which seem to me are rooted in the doctrine of salvation or redemption by propitiatory sacrifice; of imaging God as a Tribal Chieftain—and a petty one at that.

I have been informed by competent theologians that the above-mentioned doctrine is not the official teaching of the Roman Catholic Church. Rather it is a theory of atonement attributed to St. Anselm in the thirteenth century. I am most happy to learn that. Yet, I must confess it is the doctrine with which I grew up. It is the doctrine I preached for many years. It is the doctrine I heard given back to me by many men and women in their fears and anxieties. I am not in the position of an Andrew Greely to do a survey on this matter but I would wager, if I had anything to wager, that for most Catholics forty-five years and older, that is what they were taught.

Why do I make an issue of this? Simply because it illustrates in the lives of many the power of an Image of God—however implicit, subliminal, unwarranted and even blasphemous it may have been. The teachings resulting from that image engendered much fear and anxiety among so many. This is a good reason for me to make an issue of it.

Imaging God as a parent or as a Pre-K teacher of autistic and profoundly handicapped children who loves His/Her children unconditionally places the focus not on sins but rather on acceptance. This is true also of imaging the Transcendent as the One and the Many dancing the Cosmic Dance.

Sin/Darkness—Missing the Mark

We have been so accustomed to thinking of sins as intentional acts against the Law, that we tend to forget the reality of sin in our very beings, our unspiritual selves, as Paul mentions in his letter to the Romans 7:18-25:

> The fact is, I know of nothing good living in me—living, that is, in my unspiritual self—for though the will to do what is good is in me, the performance is not, with the result that instead of doing the good things I want to do, I carry out the sinful things I do not want. When I act against my will, then, it is not **my true self** doing it, but sin which lives in me.
>
> In fact, this seems to be the rule, that every single time I want to do good it is something evil that comes to hand. In my **inmost self** I dearly love God's Law, but I can see that my body follows a different law that battles against the law which my reason dictates. This is what makes me **a prisoner of that law of sin which lives inside my body.**
>
> What a wretched man I am! Who will rescue me from this body doomed to death? Thanks be to God through Jesus Christ our Lord.

In short, it is I who with my reason serve the law of God, and no less I who serve in my **unspiritual self** the law of sin [emphases mine].

Paul definitely speaks of his **inmost self** and **true self**. He also speaks of his **unspiritual self,** of that **"law of sin that lives inside"** his body; **"this body doomed to death;"** and of being **"a prisoner of that law of sin which lives inside my body."** In the first exercise of the first week of his Spiritual Exercises, Saint Ignatius invites the exercitant to use the imagination to experience what sin is: "To see in imagination **my soul as prisoner** in this corruptible body, and to consider my whole composite being as an exile here on earth, cast out to live among brute beasts. I said my whole composite being body and soul."

St. Paul says, "This is what makes me a **prisoner** of that law of sin that lives inside my body." St. Ignatius speaks of the soul as a **prisoner** in this corruptible body [emphasis mine].

Neither St. Paul nor St. Ignatius of Loyola are speaking of sins committed against any laws. They are not speaking of moral transgressions. They are speaking of Sin/Darkness—Missing the Mark; what the *Baltimore Catechism* tells us are the effects of Original Sin; that our understanding is darkened, our will is weakened, and there is in us a strong inclination to evil. This is being "oughtistic" and profoundly handicapped.

Sin/Darkness may be thought of as a mindset, such that human thinks:

(a) that human is not body and soul, but simply this rational animal that exists from the moment of conception until death and then exists no more, or

(b) that human does have a soul: that, indeed, human is created by God to know, love and serve God in this life and to be happy with God forever in heaven; and, therefore, human's existence on Planet Earth is a test. If human passes the test and does all that God wants, human goes to heaven; if human does not pass the test human exists eternally in a hell of torture and no hope, and

(c) for each of the above human has no choice in being here.

Let's Continue to Play

The result of (a) + (c) is the Law of Survival of the Fittest—the Law of Self-Preservation: "Do unto others before they do unto you." This creates fear, anxiety and the desire to have enough power over the earth, the vegetable kingdom, the so-called non-rational animal kingdom, and whatever members of the so-called rational kingdom that may be necessary for survival. Hence power structures of whatever kind are created. **Because if I do not survive I cease to be.**

The result of (b) + (c) are that human lives in a certain fear and anxiety that human may not measure up to the requirements and so be condemned to hell for eternity; this generates a certain amount of frustration and rage rooted in the feeling of powerlessness because human has no choice in the matter. It is the victimization of human.

The dynamics and resulting mental attitudes I've just described are what I have experienced in the average Catholic during my forty-five years of priesting in parishes and retreat ministry. And I must confess that, in the past, I have encouraged it by my preaching and teaching what I was taught. I maintain now that this mindset in all of its ramifications is **Sin/Darkness—Missing The Mark**. This is the prison of the corruptible body, the exile among brute beasts in which the soul finds itself. It engenders for many a feeling of impotence from which flows an anger—even rage—that is frequently unacknowledged because it is against "God." This may become the source of energy for both good and bad. We have all experienced in ourselves and others benevolence and charity rooted in the fear of not measuring up. This fear and anxiety is at the basis of the destructive, judgmental attitude of so many well-intentioned humans, as well as of so many groups in the Church and, frequently, of the Church herself. Am I making a judgement here or simply an observation? I prefer to think it is an observation. I am not condemning. I observe this with compassion for the Church, myself and all who have been caught up in this.

The **need** for survival tends to dominate our lives. We are taught from earliest years to achieve, to succeed, to compete, to win. Our cultural heroines and heroes are those who have done all of the above, received much recognition, and possibly become wealthy in the process, and thus insured survival and power. Our identification with social groups, racial groups and so on, reinforces the cycle of achievement and competition. It is through these mistaken values that we lose our souls, becoming less aware of the compassionate soul/spirit that each of us is, as made in the image and likeness of God. This is Sin/Darkness. This is being "oughtistic" and profoundly handicapped. This is the world, the principles of which, according to John, are "the sensual body, the lustful eye, pride in possessions." 1 John 2:16.

We live in this darkness and are involved in this darkness, using the tools of darkness to proclaim the light. As so frequently happens, the medium becomes the message.

Salvation by Christ the Light of the World

Opposite the need to survive is the Good News that we are essentially, in our quintessential thusness, eternal spirits and do not need to survive. This is the light that Jesus brings to us by proclaiming to us that we are children of God. Or, to put it another way, Jesus is a superb Cosmic Dancer who invites us, the many, of which He is one, to allow ourselves to be danced by the One.

> *You have learnt how it was said: You must love your neighbor and hate your enemy. But I say this to you: Love your enemies and pray for those who persecute you;* **in this way you will be children of your Father in heaven** *[emphasis mine], for He*

> *causes His sun to rise on bad men as well as good, and his rain to fall on honest and dishonest men alike....You must therefore set no bounds to your love as your Heavenly Father sets none to His.* Matthew 5:43-48

This belief that there is **sin/darkness** and there is **salvation/light** through the life, passion, death, resurrection and ascension of Jesus Christ is at the core of Catholic doctrine on salvation.

Did Jesus in fact sacrifice himself to free us from our sinfulness? Yes, of course, as the classical hero who brings light to his people and is killed by those who "have shown they prefer darkness to light" (John 3:19). From His own spiritual journey into the heights, he ascended and then descended among us to let us know that we are indeed children of God. In so doing he risked being killed by those who prefer the darkness; the kingdom of humans having power over one another and over all creation.

That Christ is the light of the world is in John's Prologue and throughout the Johannine literature very clearly. It is also in the Synoptics.

This is why He came:

> *The spirit of the Lord is upon me, for he has anointed me. He has sent me to bring the good news to the poor, to proclaim liberty to the captives and to the blind new sight, to set the downtrodden free, to proclaim the Lord's year of favour.* Luke 4:18

> *After John had been arrested, Jesus went into Galilee. There he proclaimed the Good News from God. 'The time has come,' he said, 'and the kingdom of God is close at hand. Repent, and believe the Good News.'* Mark 1:14,15

The kingdom of God is not like the kingdom of humans. Jesus came proclaiming the Good News and invites us to trust it. The good news is that the Father loves us unconditionally, and has indeed made us His children.

The Father's gift to us:

Think of the love that the Father has lavished on us, by letting us be called God's children; and that is what we are.
Because the world refused to acknowledge Him, therefore it does not acknowledge us.
My dear people, we are already the children of God, but what we are to be in the future has not yet been revealed; all we know is that when it is revealed we shall be like Him because we shall see Him as He really is. 1 John 3

Indeed, from his fullness we have, all of us, received—yes, grace in return for grace, since, though the Law was given through Moses, grace and truth have come through Jesus Christ. John 1:16, 17

All that came to be had life in Him and that life was the light of men, a light that shines in the dark, a light that darkness could not overpower. John 1:4,5

Very importantly, there is the ancient liturgical practice of the Catholic Church:

There is Advent: the waiting for the light;

There is Christmas: the people who lived in darkness have seen a great light;

There is Epiphany: Christ is the light to the gentiles;

There is the Presentation in the Temple: the light of Israel;

Then there is the struggle between light and darkness depicted in the first Sunday of Lent with the Temptations of Jesus—this struggle is depicted throughout the Lenten season;

There is the apparent victory of darkness over light in the crucifixion, but this is the death that brings life and light:

—this is celebrated in the Easter Triduum, and begins with the Mass of the Lord's Supper on Thursday.

The Lord's Passion and Death are celebrated on Good Friday. On Saturday the Easter Vigil begins with the Service of Light, in which the Paschal Candle symbolizing the risen Christ—the Light of the World—is blessed. Later in the service water is blessed for baptisms. Symbolically, the lighted Paschal Candle is dipped three times into the water indicating that all who will be baptized will be baptized (immersed) into the life of Christ, which is Light. Then some individuals may be baptized. Afterwards all present are invited to renew their baptismal promises.

In short, Christ is the Light into Whom all are immersed. There is Sin/Darkness, the not knowing who we are. There is **LIGHT**—the life, passion, death, resurrection, and ascension of Jesus by which we are invited to trust in the gift of the Father—that we are children of God.

Salvation by enlightenment is at the core of Catholic teaching and especially Catholic liturgical practice—the whole Easter celebration is the center piece of the Liturgical Year.

What does it mean to be children of God? This is an anthropomorphic expression of being the many which are expressions of the One as discussed in Part I, so that a child of God is an eternal spirit of the Eternal Spirit. Jesus reminds us to be compassionate as our heavenly Father is compassionate. May we not say that to be children of God is indeed to be Compassionate Energies dancing the Cosmic Dance? Of course this is babbling, fantasizing in the midst of mystery. This is much healthier than saying that we really know what God, we and all the energies of the Cosmos are. So let us continue to play as we remember that

WE MUST LET GO

OF EVERYTHING

WE HAVE TAKEN LITERALLY

ALL OF OUR LIVES;

ONLY THEN WILL WE BE OPEN

TO THE MYSTERY

OF THE TRANSCENDENT

WITHIN US.

PART VI

Exercises for Compassionate Energies

The following is based on the unproved and unprovable assumption that each human is both temporal and eternal. The unprovability of the assumption in no way minimizes its value, the intuition of the many of the human species through the millenia in all cultures simply knows.

The eternal dimension is called spirit or soul or cosmic consciousness or psyche, and simply is. The temporal dimension is the enfleshment of the eternal in time. The enfleshment is an ephemeral epiphany, a phenomenon, a physical manifestation of the eternal spirit. The difference is that in the temporal, the eternal spirit is limited by the physical, and takes on such limitations as gender, race, nationality, cultural characteristics of its ancestors, and the conditioning and programming of its present cultural training from the time of its conception on through its temporal life. From the perception of a cosmic consciousness one might say the eternal spirit experiences "oughtism" and profound deprivation.

Principle and Foundation for Compassionate Energies Participating in the Evolutionary Process of The Human Species

Each Compassionate Energy that freely enters into the human experience does so to be aware of, to revere, to celebrate and to be in harmony with the Transcendent Source from which it is, and thus to grow in the experience of this Transcendent Source and of itself—this Compassionate Energy.

Every other energy on Planet Earth and indeed in the Cosmos is present to aid in this noble quest.

Hence, human (enfleshed Compassionate Energy) is present to the other energies to the extent that they are an aid and withdraws from them to the extent that they are a hindrance in this noble quest.

Therefore, it is good for human to constantly seek a state of freedom; for example, preferring neither health to sickness, neither poverty to riches, neither honor to dishonor, neither a long life to a short life; seeking always to be free from being **determined** by identities such as religion, race, nationality, profession or role in life.

The one desire and choice is that which is more conducive to the noble quest for which the Compassionate Energy became human.

(N.B. It is well to consider this Principle and Foundation for a day or two, and to refer to it frequently during the following Exercises.)

Reminders

Daringly and playfully I blithely describe the wondrous mysteries that we are ! ! ! !

Persona: The persona is the collection of all those qualities of the individual imposed by gender, race, nationality, religion, both inherited and programmed into the individual by family, school, religion, society, etc. This may be called the Temporal Image and may be constantly changing as the individual establishes his or her place in society; and then further as the individual seeks her/his true self. These are the limitations the Compassionate Energy assumes upon entering the human experience.

True Self: The Higher Self; Always Self; Eternal Spirit; Soul; Compassionate Energy. That which enters into the human experience to praise, revere and serve the Source from which it is, and thus to grow in the experience of its Source and of itself. To enter into the human experience this true self must limit itself to a persona.

Sin: (hemertia—the Greek word for sin); Missing the Mark; Darkness; not knowing. It is identification with the temporal as though it were the eternal reality or as if there were no eternal reality.

Let us play! Imagine that we are indeed children of God, eternal spirits of the Eternal Spirit; that our enfleshment, incarnation, is to bring light into the darkness. But the only way we can do that is to forget that we are eternal spirit and experience what it means to be in the darkness—to be the darkness.

> We are ambassadors for Christ, God as it were appealing through us. We implore you, in Christ's name: be reconciled to God! For our sakes God made him who did not know sin to be

sin, so that in him we might become the very holiness of God. 2 Cor. 5:20-21

In your minds you must be the same as Christ Jesus; His state was divine yet he did not cling to his equality with God but emptied himself to assume the condition of a slave and became as men are. Philippians 2:5-7

Similar to the experience of Jesus of Nazareth, but in its own manner, the eternal spirit chooses to empty itself of its awareness of being essentially eternal spirit and assumes the human condition, becoming enslaved to the limitations of the persona, and thinks that it must survive as this human in time and space or simply be extinct. This, of course, brings with it the fear of death and all the anxieties about sickness and suffering that can bring about death. So the total focus of the human is to survive by whatever means. Thus, human is conditioned and becomes programmed to all the skills of individual and group survival; identifying with whatever group or value system is perceived as an aid to survival.

The Purpose of the Exercises

The following exercises are divided into three parts:

The first set of exercises is designed to help one become aware of sin/darkness on Planet Earth.

The second set of exercises is designed to help develop—with no guilt—an awareness of sin/darkness within oneself.

The third set of exercises is designed to help develop an awareness that we today, individually and collectively, are the incarnation of the Christ.

Sin/Darkness on Planet Earth

The assumption is that we humans, **as the Earth conscious of itself,**[1] are here to be aware of, to revere, to celebrate and to be in harmony with the Transcendent Source of Cosmogenesis. It may be said that when reverence for the Transcendent and the evolutionary process of the Cosmos is lacking, human has fallen into a selfish narcissism which is Sin/Darkness.

The result of Sin/Darkness is that the persona becomes so identified with or addicted to whatever in the temporal experience, it loses its soul—an awareness of and a functioning from its true self—Compassionate Energy.

The following are exercises to help me become aware of Sin/Darkness on Planet Earth. I am invited to become aware of the values that are rooted in the fallacious need to survive, both on the physical and on the persona level, which encourage the desire for riches, power, pleasure—simply living selfishly. With this value system all of one's energy goes into one's temporal persona. I am invited to contrast this with the values manifested in the crucifixion of Jesus—unselfish love, being ridiculed, being an outcast, being misunderstood, not being recognized, poverty, powerlessness and suffering. This latter is the wisdom of God. In this all the energy goes into the eternal Compassionate Love. Of course, most live in the tension between the two energies within themselves.

---

[1] Thomas Berry, Contemplation and World Order.

Suggested Format for Each Exercise

As a part of each exercise I am invited first to read the exercise, know what I am to imagine, and have some idea of what I am invited to become aware of.

Next I am invited to go into deep relaxation.

A Method for Relaxing Deeply

1. Take **time—time—time** to relax deeply. I may do this by lying down, sitting up straight, relaxing in a reclining chair or finding any other position of the body—such as the lotus position, in which I can relax deeply and go into the center of my being—in a sense, to lose track of time and be open to the eternal dimension of myself.

2. Become aware of the muscles of the body beginning with the head and going down, or beginning with the feet and going up, or beginning with the solar plexus and radiating out—whatever works for me. It is well not to get stuck on any particular method.

3. As I become aware of the muscles I am invited to allow them to relax, to grow soft like cooked pasta. They know how to do it. I am invited to allow them to do what they know how to do.

4. Imagine a glowing white light radiating from my solar plexus seeking out all of the muscles and any tense organs in my body. This white light massages each and every fiber of my being bringing relaxation and peace to my entire physical body.

5. Imagine myself going down from my conscious level to that space within myself wherein I am more in touch with the Compassionate Energy, the Eternal Spirit, the Eternal Beauty, the Eternal Love that I am. I do this by imagining

myself going down a flight of stairs counting backwards from ten or fifteen as I go down.

6. Rest in this safe, secure space for a few moments.

7. Thank God for this opportunity to be in this dimension of my being.

8. Ask God to help me to be in touch with that receptive feminine energy within me to open me to the mysteries I am now contemplating.

When I have gone down into the depths of myself and asked God to allow me to be open and receptive, I then allow my imagination to bring forward the scenes decided on or any others that may come to me; allow myself to experience whatever feelings come to me and whatever considerations emerge within me.

I am invited to make time for myself to be receptive to each and every experience, playfully and without concern for time. I am invited to remember that it is not a matter of information but a matter of experiencing as deeply as it is given to me at this time in my journey the Sin/Darkness on Planet Earth. For it is this Sin/Darkness that hinders so many from being aware that they are each eternal compassionate spirits. Hence, they radiate selfish survival energy more than the unselfish compassionate energy which each eternally is.

> *Caution:* I am invited to see myself as a cosmic consciousness. Because of my conditioning, I may get caught in the trap of examination of conscience—i.e. judging as right/wrong, good/bad, rather than simply observing what is going on on Planet Earth from the perspective of a cosmic consciousness. I am invited to **observe with deep compasson** rather than **judge** myself.

Imagery of Crucifixion

In contrast to the selfish narcissism imaged in each of the exercises, I am invited *at the end of each exercise* to image the crucifixion of Jesus of Nazareth. I allow this to become rather graphic. I remember that he is experiencing the apex of the Passover movement of the Cosmic Dance. I allow the following simply to pervade my being:

> *A crucified Christ...who is the power and wisdom of God. For God's foolishness is wiser than human wisdom, and God's weakness is stronger than human strength.* 1 Cor. 1:23-25

I then become aware of a galactic experience. My mind's eye opens and I see beyond the physical. I am aware of angels and other infinitely diverse cosmic consciousnesses and energies beyond all possibility of numbering or naming. All are gathering and gazing with loving reverence on this scene of the Transcendent's compassionate love-energy present in the dying of the persona Jesus of Nazareth.

Instantaneously, without my thinking, the meaning of Paul's hymn in the beginning of Philippians fills my being:

> *His state was divine yet he did not cling to his equality with God but emptied himself to assume the condition of a slave and became as men are; and being as all men are, he was humbler yet, even to accepting death, death on a cross.* Philippians 2:6-8.

I reflect on this mystery. This is the Passover—the movement from death to life. Jesus is one of the Many that is in the One and is called the visible image of that invisible Transcendent Compassion. He is the archetype of the compassion, courage and trust that is in each of us to dance the difficult and necessary step of Passover, moving from slavery to freedom, from death to life.

> *But God raised him high and gave him the name which is above all other names so that all beings in the heavens, on earth,*

and in the underworld, should bend the knee at the name of Jesus and that every tongue should acclaim Jesus Christ as Lord, to the glory of God the Father. Philippians 2:9-11.

He said that He and the Father are One; and prayed that we too be aware of this oneness that just as He is in the Father and the Father in Him so we are one. When accused of blasphemy for saying that He and the Father are one, He said that we too are children of God (John 10:33-34).

What is my response to this wonder—this mystery—that as He is in the Father and the Father in Him, so am I one in Them?

What is my response to this mystery that He is willing to die to be obedient to His True Self, trusting that He lives even though He dies?

After going through the exercise in the use of the imagination and whatever considerations come to me, I am then invited to write whatever I may have thought—but more importantly—**whatever I may have felt.** I may experience feelings by making comparisons. For example, I may imagine my eternal spirit as a prisoner in my body. By comparison, I may imagine myself being born and growing up in a jail cell with only one small window. What would be my experience of the outside world? What would be my feelings? Now I am invited to use crayons or paints or clay or whatever medium I dare to use to help me get more in touch with and express my feelings.

Sin Darkness on Planet Earth
First Exercise—MOTHER EARTH

1. I go through all of the relaxing exercises (pp. 61 & 62) to bring myself into deep relaxation and openness to become aware of the **mystery** I am contemplating.

2. I thank the Transcendent and the angel within me for inviting me to this time of openness and awareness.

3. I imagine myself as a cosmic consciousness out in intergalactic space. I become aware of the explosion of Tiamet, the supernova that gives birth to our Solar System. I become aware of what is to become Planet Earth. It is only in its gaseous state. This occurs about four and a half billion years ago. I see it gradually evolve over many millennia. I experience life in its simplest forms beginning in the waters of Earth. I experience over the millennia the evolution of many forms of life until there is the modern human just 40,000 years ago.

The beauty of Planet Earth almost overwhelms me. I see her towering mountains, her thunderous waterfalls, her breathtaking quiet deserts, her winding rivers, her mysterious oceans, her peaceful lakes and groves. I become aware of the multitudinous forms of life in the waters, on the land and in the air. The multiform beauty and sounds are beyond articulation.

I am amazed and in awe as I witness Earth producing all that is necessary to feed all the different species. Of course this means eating and being nourished by others. Nonetheless, all species are nourished by Her from whom they have evolved.

In these last 40,000 years I see the development of humans on different continents; the beginnings of languages, the beginnings of religions, the beginnings of nations, etc. I am aware of human's creativity in all of the arts, of human's continual progress in all of the sciences, becoming more and more conscious of the Earth of which it is the consciousness. I am aware and exhilarated as I witness beauty and compassion radiating from so many individuals of the human species.

Then I become aware that the human species in its fallacious need to survive, its fear of extinction, its Sin/Darkness, not only takes what it needs for immediate survival but becomes very greedy in taking more than it needs. I witness the more powerful tribes, then nations taking more than they need and reducing others to slavery. I witness the industrial nations or industrialists stripping forests and destroying Earth in many other ways just for their own monetary gain and their own pleasure and convenience during their short stay on Mother Earth—from whom they ultimately evolved.

I become aware of the Sin/Darkness in which the individuals of the human species live focused as they are on their own separateness, their own individual needs for physical and persona survival. I become aware of their living in fear of death for themselves and their loved ones. I become aware of the anxiety and great stress in which many live, in trying to live up to the expectations of others and of themselves, as they have been taught. I am aware that because of all of this they have little time or inclination to being present to the life of Mother Earth.

I am saddened and confused and in awe as I witness the compassion and the beauty in tension with this selfish narcissism.

4. I contemplate cosmic consciousnesses gazing on the crucifixion as described above. (pp. 63 & 64)

5. Now I write or draw pictures or paint or use clay or whatever to get in touch with and to express my feelings.

6. I then take time to thank God, or my angel, or my eternal spirit for the experience.

I am invited to do the same for each one of the exercises. Obviously it is unwise to do this all in one day. I may possibly do it once or twice a day for an hour or so. There is no timeline. There is no need to finish anything. For example, I may take the first exercise on Mother Earth, and read sections—or all—of the book, *The Universe Story,* or some such book. And to become more aware of the life, passion, death, resurrection and ascension of Jesus of Nazareth, I may decide to read the Gospel according to one of the Evangelists, straight through as though I were reading a short story—putting aside all that I have been taught—simply to acquaint myself with the life of the man, Jesus of Nazareth.

Sin Darkness on Planet Earth
Second Exercise: SHOPPING MALL

1. I am invited to go into deep relaxation as suggested above. (pp. 61 & 62)

2. I thank the Transcendent and the angel within me for inviting me to this time of openness and awareness.

3. I am invited to imagine myself walking through any shopping mall and simply to become aware of—i.e. to observe—the persons shopping, the merchants, the merchandise, the advertising; realizing that advertising develops a need, hence a desire that can cause an unhealthy tension and even violence within and between individuals.

I become aware of the materialism of our culture and the effect this has on our values. "What gain, then, is it for a man to win the whole world and ruin his life?" Mk. 8:37

Questions:

To what extent do I observe compassion, love and reverence in this?

To what extent do I observe the need for physical survival, the desire for the temporal survival and exaltation of the persona (ego)?

To what extent do I observe the exaltation of competition, success, power over others?

4. Next I allow myself to contemplate the crucifixion, followed immediately by the galactic scene as given above. (pp. 63 & 64)

5. After going through this exercise with the use of the imagination and whatever considerations come to me in the final contemplation of the crucifixion and the galactic scene, I am then invited to write whatever I may have thought, but **more importantly, whatever I may have felt.** Now I am invited to use crayons, or paints or clay or whatever medium I dare to use, to help me get more in touch with and express my feelings.

6. I then take time to thank God, or my angel, or my eternal spirit for the experience.

Sin Darkness on Planet Earth
Third Exercise: HEROES AND HEROINES

1. I am invited to go into deep relaxation as suggested above (pp. 61 & 62).

2. I thank the Transcendent and the angel within me for inviting me to this time of openness and awareness.

3. I am invited to be aware of the heroes and heroines in the political, business, sports, entertainment, and even religious worlds; how many are rewarded for their spirit of competition, their hard work, their success.

Questions:

To what extent do I observe compassion, love and reverence in this?

To what extent do I observe the need for physical survival, the desire for the temporal survival and exaltation of the persona (ego)?

To what extent do I observe the exaltation of competition, success, power over others?

4. Next I allow myself to contemplate the crucifixion followed immediately by the galactic scene as given above (pp. 63 & 64).

5. After going through this exercise with the use of the imagination and whatever considerations come to me in the final contemplation of the crucifixion and the galactic scene, I am then invited to write whatever I may have thought, but **more importantly, whatever I may have felt.** Now I am invited to use crayons, or paints or clay or

whatever medium I dare to use, to help me get more in touch with and express my feelings.

6. I then take time to thank God or my angel or my eternal spirit for the experience.

Sin Darkness on Planet Earth
Fourth Exercise: ADVERTISEMENTS

1. I am invited to go into deep relaxation as suggested above. (pp. 61 & 62)

2. I thank the Transcendent and the angel within me for inviting me to this time of openness and awareness.

3. I am invited to be aware of advertisements in newspapers, magazines, TV, billboards, etc.

Questions:

To what extent do I observe compassion, love and reverence in this?

To what extent do I observe the need for physical survival, the desire for the temporal survival, and exaltation of the persona (ego)?

To what extent do I observe the exaltation of competition, success, power over others?

4. Next I allow myself to contemplate the crucifixion followed immediately by the galactic scene as given above (pp. 63 & 64).

5. After going through this exercise with the use of the imagination and whatever considerations come to me in the final contemplation of the crucifixion and the galactic scene, I am then invited to write whatever I may have thought, but **more importantly, whatever I may have felt.** Now I am invited to use crayons, or paints or clay or whatever medium I dare to use, to help me get more in touch with and express my feelings.

6. I then take time to thank God or my angel or my eternal spirit for the experience.

Sin Darkness on Planet Earth
Fifth Exercise: NEWS AND MEDIA

1. I am invited to go into deep relaxation as suggested above. (pp. 61 & 62).

2. I thank the Transcendent and the angel within me for inviting me to this time of openness and awareness.

3. I am invited to become aware of people in the news and in the media—ethnic, racial, national, religious and political identities. Then, I am invited to be aware of the strife among these identities.

Questions:

To what extent do I observe compassion, love and reverence in this?

To what extent do I observe the need for physical survival, the desire for the temporal survival, and exaltation of the persona (ego)?

To what extent do I observe the exaltation of competition, success, power over others?

4. Next I allow myself to contemplate the crucifixion followed immediately by the galactic scene as given above (pp. 63 & 64).

5. After going through this exercise with the use of the imagination and whatever considerations come to me in the final contemplation of the crucifixion and the galactic scene, I am then invited to write whatever I may have thought, but **more importantly, whatever I may have felt.** Now I am invited to use crayons, or paints or clay or

whatever medium I dare to use, to help me get more in touch with and express my feelings.

6. I then take time to thank God or my angel or my eternal spirit for the experience.

Sin Darkness on Planet Earth
Sixth Exercise: HELL ON EARTH?

1. I am invited to go into deep relaxation as suggested above (pp. 61 & 62).

2. I thank the Transcendent and the angel within me for inviting me to this time of openness and awareness.

3. I am invited to become aware of what so many humans experience on Planet Earth. In the darkness of not knowing that they are eternal spirits they experience a sort of hell. This hell is full of fear, anxiety, physical and mental torture of every kind, a lack of hope, a not knowing God or my true self. It is full of despair. It is power over and powerlessness; it is the oppressor and the oppressed. It is the fear of sickness, poverty and death. It is battered children and women. It is ethnic cleansing. It is religious wars. It is slavery of every kind in the human experience. It is addiction of every kind, including the addiction to religious perfection. Ultimately, it is a lack of knowing that I am an eternal spirit of the Eternal Spirit or, in human terms, a child of God.

Questions:

To what extent do I observe compassion, love and reverence in this?

To what extent do I observe the need for physical survival, the desire for the temporal survival, and exaltation of the persona (ego)?

To what extent do I observe the exaltation of competition, success, power over others?

4. Next I allow myself to contemplate the crucifixion followed immediately by the galactic scene as given above (pp. 63 & 64).

5. After going through this exercise with the use of the imagination and whatever considerations come to me in the final contemplation of the crucifixion and the galactic scene, I am then invited to write whatever I may have thought, but **more importantly, whatever I may have felt.** Now I am invited to use crayons, or paints or clay or whatever medium I dare to use, to help me get more in touch with and express my feelings.

6. I then take time to thank God or my angel or my eternal spirit for the experience.

Exercises for Becoming Aware of The Sin/Darkness In My Persona

These exercises are for becoming **aware** of the **Sin/Darkness** in my life and how the darkness on the planet is in me.

Personal Sin may be described as the persona becoming attached to, addicted to, identified with whatever: the "whatever" takes the persona out of harmony with its eternal spirit. This brings about a separation in degrees—even totally so—from the awareness of the eternal spirit which it essentially is.

These exercises are designed to help me become **aware** of my own life history: of the manner in which I have been conditioned and programmed by the Sin/Darkness on Planet Earth, as experienced in the first exercises on sin.

PLEASE NOTE: In performing these exercises I am invited to listen to the story of my persona from the depths of compassion. It is important to **avoid comparisons, avoid judgments,** and **avoid the need to understand** while doing this.[2]

---

[2] Cf W. Brough Joy, M.D., *Joy's Way* (Los Angeles: J. P. Tarcher, Inc.) 1979, p. 59.

Contemplating Calvary

The following is used in the appropriate place in each one of the following exercises:

Complete the exercise by contemplating Jesus on the Cross on Calvary, allowing this to be very graphic and allowing the following to simply pervade my being;

> *A crucified Christ...who is the power and wisdom of God. For God's foolishness is wiser than human wisdom, and God's weakness is stronger than human strength.*

I experience myself in a soft meadow surrounded by every sort of imaginable flower, tree, shrub. Far and near I experience rolling hills and snow-capped mountains and thunderous waterfalls cascading from unseen heights. I seem to be the center of attention of a cosmic dance of every sort of animal; every imaginable and unimaginable winged creature; every imaginable and unimaginable cosmic consciousness and angel. All are in soft yet vivid hues of every color that is or that can be. **All celebrate me for I too have emptied myself of an awareness of my eternal spirit and have become a slave to my persona, as all humans are, to bring compassion into the human experience.**

I experience the Transcendent Source of the Cosmos gazing on me through all of creation with unconditional love and compassion.

In the midst of these wonders is Jesus of Nazareth, the Supreme Cosmic Dancer, with the wounds in His hands, feet and side glowing gloriously. He encourages me to be in touch with my energies of courage, strength and trust, which empower me to go through the continual passovers of my life as did He.

Instantaneously, without my thinking, the meaning of Paul's hymn in the beginning of Philippians fills me:

> *His state was divine yet he did not cling to his equality with God, but emptied himself to assume the condition of a slave and became as men are; and being as all men are, he was humbler yet, even to accepting death, death on a cross. But God raised him high and gave him the name which is above all other names so that* **all beings** *in the heavens, on earth, and in the underworld, should bend the knee at the name of Jesus and that every tongue should acclaim Jesus Christ as Lord, to the glory of God the Father.*

He said that He and the Father are one, and when accused of blasphemy said that we too are children of God.

Then simply thank Him for inviting us, me, into the light of what we, I, am; empowering me by this enlightenment to be the compassionate, unconditional love that I am. Then become aware of what He suffered to do this for me.

What is my response to this wonder—this mystery—that as He is in the Father and the Father in Him, so am I one in them?

Sin Darkness in My Persona
First Exercise: PLACES

1. I am invited to go into deep relaxation, as suggested above (pp. 61 & 62).

2. I thank the Transcendent and the angel within me for inviting me to this time of openness and awareness.

3. I am invited to be aware of the **places** in which I have lived, worked, gone to school, etc. It is well to take time with each place allowing oneself to imagine the place: the texture of the place, its lightness or darkness; its scent. Allow all of my senses to bring the place as fully as possible into my present consciousness, and to do this for each place. It may help not only to write the names of the places, but also to draw each of them as the little child in me would love to do, and then to color them.

As I am in these places I allow myself to be aware of the feelings which emerge into my consciousness. What happened to me in these places? There may be feelings of joy or fear, peace or anxiety, diffidence or confidence or whatever. What did this mean to me in my life? Now I allow myself to be *compassionate* to my own self as I listen to my story and become in touch with my persona as it was experiencing life in those times and places.

Questions:

To what extent do I observe compassion, love and reverence in this?

To what extent do I observe the need for physical survival, the desire for the temporal survival and exaltation of the persona (ego)?

To what extent do I observe the exaltation of competition, success and power over others?

4. Next, I am invited to contemplate Calvary, followed immediately by the cosmic scene (pp. 79 & 80).

5. After going through the exercise with the use of the imagination and whatever considerations come to me in the contemplation of Calvary and the galactic scene, I am then invited to write whatever I may have thought, but **more importantly, whatever I may have felt.** Now I am invited to use crayons or paints or clay or whatever medium I dare to use to help me get more in touch with and express my feelings.

6. I then take time to thank God or my angel or my eternal spirit for the experience.

Sin Darkness in My Persona
Second Exercise: PERSONS

1. I am invited to go into deep relaxation, as suggested above (pp. 61 & 62).

2. I thank the Transcendent and the angel within me for inviting me to this time of openness and awareness.

3. I am invited then to be aware of the **persons** who were in each of those **places** remembered. It is well to take time with each person allowing oneself to fully imagine the person. Is the person tall or short, dark or light? Do I remember the sound of a laugh, a tone of voice a special scent? Allow all of my senses to bring the person as fully as possible into my present consciousness, and to do this for each person. I write down their names and any few words that come to me that would describe the person and the relationship that was there between us.

As I am aware of these persons I allow myself to be aware of the feelings which emerge into my consciousness. What happened to me in these relationships? There may be feelings of joy or fear, peace or anxiety, diffidence or confidence or whatever. What did this mean to me in my life? Now I allow myself to be *compassionate* to my own self as I listen to my story and become in touch with my persona as it was experiencing life within those relationships.

Questions:

To what extent do I observe compassion, love and reverence in this?

To what extent do I observe the need for physical survival, the desire for the temporal survival and exaltation of the persona (ego)?

To what extent do I observe the exaltation of competition, success and power over others?

4. Next, I am invited to contemplate Calvary, followed immediately by the cosmic scene (pp. 79 & 80).

5. After going through the exercise with the use of the imagination and whatever considerations come to me in the contemplation of Calvary and the galactic scene, I am then invited to write whatever I may have thought, but **more importantly, whatever I may have felt.** Now I am invited to use crayons or paints or clay or whatever medium I dare to use to help me get more in touch with and express my feelings.

6. I then take time to thank God or my angel or my eternal spirit for the experience.

Sin Darkness in My Persona
Third Exercise: EVENTS

1. I am invited to go into deep relaxation, as suggested above (pp. 61 & 62).

2. I thank the Transcendent and the angel within me for inviting me to this time of openness and awareness.

3. I am invited to be aware of the **events** that occurred in these **places** with these **persons,** or indeed by myself. It is well to take time to allow oneself to fully imagine each event. I use all of my senses to bring each event as fully as possible into my present consciousness. It may help to give a name to each event and also to draw each of them as the little child in me would love to do, and then to color them.

As I am aware now of these events I allow myself to be aware of the feelings which emerge into my consciousness. What happened to me in these events? There may be feelings of joy or fear, peace or anxiety, diffidence or confidence or whatever. What have these events meant to me in my life? Now I allow myself to be *compassionate* to my own self as I listen to my story and become in touch with my persona as it experienced life.

Questions:

To what extent do I observe compassion, love and reverence in this?

To what extent do I observe the need for physical survival, the desire for the temporal survival and exaltation of the persona (ego)?

To what extent do I observe the exaltation of competition, success and power over others?

4. Next, I am invited to contemplate Calvary, followed immediately by the cosmic scene (pp. 79 & 80).

5. After going through the exercise with the use of the imagination and whatever considerations come to me in the contemplation of Calvary and the galactic scene, I am then invited to write whatever I may have thought, but **more importantly, whatever I may have felt.** Now I am invited to use crayons or paints or clay or whatever medium I dare to use to help me get more in touch with and express my feelings.

6. I then take time to thank God or my angel or my eternal spirit for the experience.

Sin Darkness in My Persona
Fourth Exercise: FEELINGS

1. I am invited to go into deep relaxation, as suggested above (pp. 61 & 62).

2. I thank the Transcendent and the angel within me for inviting me to this time of openness and awareness.

3. I am invited to take time to experience the **feelings** engendered by these **places, persons** and **events** as evoked in the first three exercises together and/or separately. I allow myself to be *compassionate* to my own self as I listen to my story and become in touch with my persona as it experienced life.

This is the time to freely use drawings and colorings. This enables me not only to observe with **no judgments, no comparisons and without the** *need* **to understand,** but also to get inside the person being observed; to empathize with that person, to have great compassion for that person, and to love that person unconditionally. In a very real sense it is my soul, my eternal spirit, that is observing my temporal persona—my ego.

Questions:

To what extent do I observe compassion, love and reverence in this?

To what extent do I observe the need for physical survival, the desire for the temporal survival and exaltation of the persona (ego)?

To what extent do I observe the exaltation of competition, success and power over others?

4. Next, I am invited to contemplate Calvary, followed immediately by the cosmic scene (pp. 70 & 71).

5. After going through the exercise with the use of the imagination and whatever considerations come to me in the contemplation of Calvary and the galactic scene, I am then invited to write whatever I may have thought, but **more importantly, whatever I may have felt.** Now I am invited to use crayons or paints or clay or whatever medium I dare to use to help me get more in touch with and express my feelings.

6. I then take time to thank God or my angel or my eternal spirit for the experience.

Sin Darkness in My Persona
Fifth Exercise: FAMILY

1. I am invited to go into deep relaxation, as suggested above (pp. 61 & 62).

2. I thank the Transcendent and the angel within me for inviting me to this time of openness and awareness.

3. With great compassion I allow myself to become aware of my biological family—my parents, grandparents, etc. I am encouraged to look at family photographs and other family memorabilia to help me to be deeply in touch with my gene pool.

To the extent that I am able, I allow myself to become aware of the **places, persons, events** and **feelings** in each of their lives; how each may have been conditioned and programmed by these, and how in turn I have been conditioned and programmed by them. I remember to be *compassionate* as I listen to my story and theirs as I get in touch with my persona as it experienced life.

All of this reflection has to be put into the larger picture of their race, their nationalities, their religious affiliation, their social and political situation, indeed their whole culture—for it is within this that the temporary and permanent values of right and wrong, good and bad, true and false are developed in the distant past and then gradually assumed as absolutes. By these have they been conditioned and programmed, and so have I. This is my **growing-up security**, which can become the **darkness (sin)** to which I become addicted and **enslaved**. (The religious bondage described in Parts III & V plays a part in this.) I do all of this so that from another perspective I can get in touch with my own life history.

Questions:

To what extent do I observe compassion, love and reverence in this?

To what extent do I observe the need for physical survival, the desire for the temporal survival and exaltation of the persona (ego)?

To what extent do I observe the exaltation of competition, success and power over others?

4. Next, I am invited to contemplate Calvary, followed immediately by the cosmic scene (pp. 79 & 80).

5. After going through the exercise with the use of the imagination and whatever considerations come to me in the contemplation of Calvary and the galactic scene, I am then invited to write whatever I may have thought, but **more importantly, whatever I may have felt**. Now I am invited to use crayons or paints or clay or whatever medium I dare to use to help me get more in touch with and express my feelings.

6. I then take time to thank God or my angel or my eternal spirit for the experience.

Now...

LET US PLAY ! ! !

IN THE BEGINNING BEFORE THE

BEGINNING GOD LIVES IN TOTAL

DARKNESS. THEN GOD COMES TO AN

EXPERIENCE OF GODSELF; LOVES GODSELF;

EMBRACES GODSELF AND FROM THIS

INFINITE EMBRACE IMPLODES-EXPLODES

THE COSMIC DANCE

ETERNALLY EVOLVINGLY

LOVINGLY CREATIVELY CREATING

LIGHT-LIFE-LOVE-ENERGY-SPIRIT-CHRIST

FROM WHICH WE HAVE ALL COME

AND WHICH EACH OF US IS.

Annunciation and Incarnation Year Zero A.D.

Introduction: The Annunciation of the Angel Gabriel to Mary, her visit to Elizabeth and her Magnificat are narrated in the Gospel of Luke 1:26-56. I am invited to read these passages, keeping in mind the following interpretation:

The Annunciation is the archetype of becoming aware of the Divine (Transcendent within).

Mary is the archetype of the receptive, trusting, nourishing feminine within all, both male and female.

The Angel is the archetype of those stirrings that take place within us inviting us to be aware of the Divine within us.

The "not knowing man" is not being determined or controlled by anyone, any belief system, outside myself.

Jesus is the archetype of the masculine, the focused attention of compassionate presence, of the Christness in both male and female.

Joseph, like Abraham, is the archetype of the person of Trust.

We Are the Incarnation of the Christ

Prologue: Imagine the Transcendent in inter-galactic space as three intense energies whirling in and out of one another. For our purposes we will call them One, Two and Three, though there is no order of precedence. We imagine them thinking and speaking gently and full of compassion.

One says, *"I have been looking at Planet Earth and have become concerned about the evolutionary process of the human species. Individually many are caught up in a sort of selfish narcissism. The eternal spirit, compassionate energy, animating each individual seems to become so caught up in the temporal persona each is animating that the concerns of survival of the temporal persona take over. The individual is blinded by this fallacious need to survive and lives in fear of what they call 'dying.'"*

Three: *"I agree. What misery they live in: power struggles between individuals, between races and nationalities and even between religions which they have formed to please us. They live in such a hell."*

Two: *"I will take on a human persona and proclaim to them that they, though many, are one in us. Or, to use their human images, that they are all children of God."*

Three: *"I will be near you for you must remember that to become as they are you must do as they have done and empty yourself of your divinity."*

One: *"The powers among them will not like what you say. You may have to undergo human suffering. We will be with you even though you may not experience or remember our presence."*

The three become present to Mary in Nazareth of Galilee.

We Are the Incarnation of the Christ

Annunciation and Incarnation in the Year Zero A.D.

I relax deeply, being aware of stillness. I imagine the scenes as though I am there seeing Mary and the Angel in the room in which this event takes place. I am aware of my feelings as I experience the interaction of Mary and the Angel. I do the same as I walk with Mary to visit Elizabeth and as I listen to Mary proclaim her magnificat.

After the experience I write down, or draw a picture of, what I have experienced.

I may take some time—even days or weeks—to read any one of the Evangelists Matthew, Mark, Luke or John, proclaim the life and message of Jesus of Nazareth, the good news that we are children of God, Compassionate Energies. Then I may take some time to reflect **compassionately** on the necessary development of organized religions whose purpose is to proclaim the good news. I reflect **compassionately** as I experience well-intentioned individuals in these organized religions getting caught up in the need to organize, and in the need to understand and control the proclamation of the Good News. For the sake of survival there is the desire to have social standing and political power within the religious organization. There is also the desire to have power among other religious and political organizations. This is not wrong. This is simply a dimension of the human experience. This invites me to be compassionate as my heavenly Mother/Father is compassionate.

We Are the Incarnation of the Christ

Annunciation and Incarnation in the Year 199?

First Part:
I allow myself to go into deep relaxation, then:

Imagine the time is the present on Planet Earth, 199? years after the birth of Jesus of Nazareth. The scene is in galactic space with the Transcendent imaged as the Father; The Holy Spirit appearing in diaphanous crystalline white, exquisitely feminine; and Jesus of Nazareth. Near and far are vague images of humans and angels and other cosmic energies. The Father calls Jesus of Nazareth to Him.

Father: Son, a moment ago, but 199? years ago calculated in Earth time, we looked down on Planet Earth and saw what a mess the human species was in. The eternal spirits we created and then enfleshed in the human species had forgotten where they had come from and that they were eternal. Instead, they identified with time and space. They identified with what they call races, nationalities, cultures and religions, all for the sake of survival on Planet Earth and, even worse, for the sake of pleasing **Me.** This caused them to be stressed out trying to live up to the demands of their identities. They were living in a sort of what they call "hell."

Jesus: And so we decided, with the inspiration of the Holy Spirit, that I should go there, become one of them, and remind them that they are one in us as I am in You and You in me.

Father: Look at the mess they're in now. It doesn't seem to have changed much. **So, Son, please tell me just one**

more time...what is it you say you told those people down there??

Jesus: Daddy, it's a problem.

Father: I know it's a problem. Maybe you can shed a little light on it for me.

Jesus: I'll try. But I assure you it is tough to be human. I really became human; I emptied myself of my Divinity and became a slave to those identities as all humans are. For a long while all of my energy went into that. Gradually, through long periods of what they call meditation, I began to be aware of the Eternal Spirit that I Am.

Father: Thank you.

Jesus: You're welcome. I realized that each and all of them are Your children. I told them that they were the light of the world. I told them to be compassionate just as You are compassionate. It's simply their nature to be compassionate because they are Your children.

Father: Why can't they accept that?

Jesus: Daddy, it's hard to realize. They get so involved in surviving and in being somebody in their time and space that they have no time and energy to stop and be present to their eternal spirit.

Father: What about the churches? The religions?

Jesus: The same thing happens with them. They get so involved in their programs for getting the message across, they forget the message. After a while the media—the churches—

the religions—the programs—the schools—all of the well-intentioned media, become the message.

Father: Whew! What a problem.

(There is a long pause....)

Father: While we're on the subject, how did they get this idea about a propitiatory sacrifice—that all you physically suffered is to satisfy my infinite justice? That's the damnedest thing I've ever heard.

Jesus: Daddy, I know how that must hurt you. I know you are not offended by anything they do. You just feel sorry for them. But they have in their heads that if a petty tribal chieftain or a king can be offended—and his or her dignity or justice must be satisfied—then so must yours.

Father: You mean they compare **ME** to some petty chiefain or king or even an emperor?

Jesus: Yes, Daddy, they used to put a lot of importance on kings and emperors. Why, when I let my light and power shine and enabled them to be compassionate by sharing their loaves and fishes, they wanted to make me a king. I had to run and hide.

(The Father and Jesus laugh)

Father: (To the Holy Spirit) Spirit of Mine, where do we go from here?

Holy Spirit: (Addressing herself to Jesus) Yes, it is rough being in the human experience. I was with you all the while as you came to realize. One of human's biggest problems is that they want to hold on to all that they have structured; all that they can understand. It becomes a real impediment to the next moment in their process.

Jesus: I tried to tell them that you can't put new wine into old wine skins or mend old cloth with new. I suppose they just like the security of the old and the familiar.

Holy Spirit: Now is the time for the Second Coming; to invite each one to become aware of the Transcendent, the Spark of the Divine that is in each. **If they can accept this there will indeed by a Compassionate Presence over the whole of Planet Earth.**

Father and Jesus: Amen to that!

Allow yourself to be present to whatever comes to you from the above experience.

We Are the Incarnation of the Christ

Second Part:
The Annunciation to Me:

I allow myself to go into deep relaxation, then:

I imagine the angel appearing to myself:

What is happening? Am I walking or driving or jogging or swimming? Maybe I am just snoozing or sleeping, or even meditating. What is it that enables me to be centered deep within myself?

Perhaps I am frightened and the angel says to me, "Don't be afraid. I have been with you for a long time, ever since your conception and beyond. But you don't remember that experience."

What do I say? "Are you really an angel? Have you really been with me all this time? And if so, why are you appearing to me now?"

And the angel says, "The time has come in your earthly journey for you to remember, to be made aware of the fact that you are an eternal spirit of The Eternal Spirit, a child of God: therefore, at the core of your being your very nature is compassionate love, as God is Compassionate Love." I may say something like, "If that is so, why haven't I been aware of this all along?"

And the angel says, "You don't remember, but that was part of the decision you made when you entered into the human experience. You agreed to be dominated by the absolute need to survive, with the consequent fear of death, and the need to identify with others to insure survival. Failure to live up to the expectations of others caused anxieties."

"So, what do I do now?"

"Allow yourself to be aware of what you really are," the angel says. "Allow yourself to be more and more conscious of the fact that you are indeed eternal spirit, that you have no need to survive. Then simply allow the compassionate love that you are to radiate to others."

"That's it?"

"That's it," says the angel. "And when you do that your persona gradually becomes more in harmony with your eternal spirit, and the Cosmic Dance goes a bit more smoothly."

"My spirit rejoices in the Cosmic Dance."

Reflections on the Kingdom of God

The Kingdom of God is that in which there is no king, no territory, no subjects, no laws, no sanctions.

So instead of speaking of the Kingdom of God let's use the term **Movement of the Eternal Spirit,** or, **Cosmic Dance.**

Movement of the Eternal Spirit

Incarnation, salvation, the kingdom of God, the Cosmic Dance, are realized when each of us goes within. We become one with our eternal spirit, imposing nothing on anyone and making no demands of anyone. We are simply a compassionate presence to each and all as individually and collectively we go through this journey of the human experience, and even of the planetary experience. This is the experience of transcendent unity.

Jesus speaks of this interior growth when He says:

> The kingdom of heaven is like a mustard seed which a man took and sowed in his field. It is the smallest of all the seeds, but when it is grown it is the biggest shrub of all and becomes a tree so that the birds of the air can come and shelter in its branches.

and

> The kingdom of heaven is like the yeast a woman took and mixed in with three measures of flour till it was leavened all through. Matthew 13:31-33

Thomas Berry says, "That contemplation whereby man sinks deep into the subjectivity of his own being is a primary way of experiencing the totality of things and of so constituting a truly functioning world order. This is the order of interior communion not the order of external manipulation or compulsion.[3]

The Kingdom of Man

Primarily the Kingdom of Man is an experience of our separateness from one another and the Transcendent. With the Kingdom of Man comes the instinct to survive individually and collectively. Survival is encouraging power over others, competition and success in fields of endeavor on both the physical and ego/persona levels.

These are the Social, Political and Economic dimensions of the human experience. In these dimensions there is the need for external authority with the power to teach, legislate, specify morality and, of course, set sanctions for transgressors with the power to enforce the sanctions.

The Kingdom of Man and the Cosmic Dance meet in the heart of every human. The invitation is to be aware of each, and to give each its proper value. The Kingdom of human is the Darkness only when it is not enlightened by "that life that was the light of humans, a light that shines in the dark, a light that darkness could not overpower" (John 1:4-5).

We cannot bring peace to the world. We **can be at peace,** in harmony with the Cosmic Dance, within ourselves and thus radiate this peace and harmony to others. Gradually an authentic peace may pervade. Of course this is idealistic, but we can live in hope and compassionate presence as we journey together.

---

[3] Thomas Berry, *Contemplation and World Order.*

We Are the Incarnation of the Christ

Meditation on the Movement of the Cosmic Dance.

For this meditation on the Kingdom of God—or the Movement of the Cosmic Dance—I am invited to go into deep relaxation, as suggested above (pp. 61 & 62).

I am invited to ask that I be very open to whatever the Transcendent or my angel or my eternal spirit wishes me to receive at this time.

In this relaxed and receptive state I bring to mind the parable of Jesus: *"The kingdom of heaven is like the yeast a woman took and mixed in with three measures of flour till it was leavened all through"* (Matthew 13:33).

I am invited:

to imagine the yeast being mixed with the flour:
to imagine the yeast as a living organism which lives and grows rapidly with the gluten in the flour;
to imagine the whole being leavened;
to imagine the whole being punched down, rising again and being punched down, rising again and being punched down; being made into loaves;
rising and being put into the oven wherein the heat kills the yeast.
From this comes bread by which we are nourished

The Kingdom of God, Compassionate Energies dancing the Cosmic Dance, is like the yeast. The Compassionate Energy that each of us is, when allowed to mix into the whole, leavens the whole—dies and rises and gives life to the whole. This is another dimension of the passover movement of the Cosmic Dance.

After going through this exercise with the use of the imagination and whatever considerations come to me in this contemplation, I am invited to write whatever I may have thought, but **more importantly, whatever I may have felt.** I may experience feelings by making comparisons. Now I am invited to use crayons or paints or clay or whatever medium I dare to use to help me get more in touch with and express my feelings.

I then take time to thank God or my angel or my eternal spirit for the experience.

I may also take other parables on the Kingdom from the fourth chapter of Mark and the thirteenth chapter of Matthew. In using the parables that have to do with seeds, it may be well to remember that when a seed goes through the germination process, it seems to die to its former self in the shell, but a seed "don't die dead, it dies live." Again, this is another example of the Passover Movement of the Cosmic Dance.

The Call to Compassionate Presence
by Julie A. LeBourgeois

The miracle of Easter
   is neither the cross nor the empty tomb,
     but the multiple appearances
        of the risen Lord
           among the living—among the dead -
           on roadways—on waterways -
           to those whose faith is reeling -
           to those whose world is out of sync.

The resurrection brings him back again,
   unfettered by the bonds
     of time and place,
     of near and far,
     of life and death.

He is with us, Alleluia!
He is with us in the holy here and now,
   no longer forced
     to portion out his time
        among the pressing multitudes.

We, too, have been transformed
   into an Easter people.
We have, in fact, become
   the new Temple of God,
   the new Ark of the Covenant,
   the new Compassionate Presence
      in a world that is loved, but knows it not;
      a world that is saved, but savors it not;
      a world that is full of joy, but rejoices not.

He is with us forever,
　　and because he is
　　human life will never be the same.
This, then, is the message, the meaning, and the miracle
　　of that tremendous Eastertide
　　　　sometimes known as life.

AMEN! ALLELUIA

the end

APPENDIX
Thomas Berry

The following is from an essay by Thomas Berry on Contemplation and World Order (reproduced with kind permission of the author).

"Man is discovering anew his place within the earth process. He begins to realize that he is not lord of the universe. He depends on the dynamics of the earth to sustain him in his own being and in all his activities. Man must define himself primarily in relation to the earth, not primarily in himself. Man is the consciousness of the earth. The earth in this context becomes the primary subject; man a mode of earth being. This is the new human situation. But once this adjustment of his center of attribution is established, man can then deal with the problem of order.

"It is within this context that I would like to situate the type of contemplation that can be effective in assisting toward world order. The first thing to note is that the primary spiritual journey is not the journey of the individual soul to the divine, nor is it the journey of the Christian people, nor is it the journey of the human community, it is the journey of the primordial energy as it has taken shape as the universe has moved toward its highest expression. More immediately it is the journey of the planet earth from the time it took shape out of the stardust (when the solar system was formed), formed itself into a ball of molten elements, and then produced its topography through the course of some billions of years. Once this was achieved the multitude of plant and animal forms took shape in the sea, on the land and in the air, until finally man and the world we see about us came into being. At each level of emergence a higher spiritual mode of expression was achieved until a fullness of consciousness appeared in man. Now we experience the great journey of man to the fullness of his human mode of being.

"From that moment, some two million years ago, the entire earth process has been gradually altered under the influence of its most powerful single force, consciousness. But the power of consciousness did not begin to reach its full effect until the technological age appeared and the human system let loose its destructive powers upon the rest of the earth. Now we see that the human life system is integral with the total set of life systems, that the world order is truly the world order and not simply a human order, that man must accept himself in his functional role and submit to the dominance of the whole.

"This is the context of contemplation. Man is that being in whom the earth reflects on itself. The assumption of this earth mode of consciousness is the primary step toward a contemplation that will be effective in our present situation.

"The second consequence of our contemplation should be functional awareness of the primacy of subjective communion with the world over objective manipulation of the world. One of the great achievements of man during the early period of awakened consciousness was his capacity for subjective communion with the totality of things and with each particular thing. Each fragment of matter had its own subjectivity, its own interiority, its own spirit presence. It was to this spirit presence that man addressed himself. So with the trees and flowers, birds and animals, so with the wind and sea and the stars, so with the sun and moon. In all things there was a self, a subjectivity, a center; man communed with this center with a profound intimacy.

"That contemplation whereby man sinks deep into the subjectivity of his own being is a primary way of experiencing the totality of things and of so constituting a truly functional world order. This is the order of interior communion not the order of external manipulation or compulsion. Each aspect of reality is discovered in this mutual indwelling which is the supreme art of life. Nothing can be itself without being in communion with everything else, nor can anything truly be the other without first acquiring a capacity for interior presence to itself. These come together in some mysterious way. Thus the deepening of the personal center becomes the deepening of the capacity for communion. Since all things gravitate toward each other, man has only to permit the inner movements of his own being to establish his universal presence to all the earth."

Thomas Merton

Thomas Merton's commentary on the **Bhagavad-Gita** *is from his essay, "The Significance of the* **Bhagavad-Gita** *printed as appendix IX in the 1973 edition of his* **Asian Journal.**

"It is important for the Western reader to situate the *Gita* in its right place. Whereas the Upanishads contemplate the unconditioned, formless Brahma, the Godhead beyond created existence and beyond personality, the *Gita* deals with brahman under the conditioned form and name of Krishna. There is no 'I-Thou' relationship with the unconditioned Brahma, since there can be no conceivable subject-object division or interpersonal division in him, at least according to Hindu thought. In Christianity, too, the Godhead is above and beyond all distinction of persons. The Flemish and Rhenish mystics described it as beyond all form, distinction and division. Unconditioned Brahma, the Godhead, is not 'what we see,' it is 'who sees.' 'Thou art that.' Unconditioned brahman is pure consciousness. Pure Act—but not activity. Conditioned brahman is the 'Maker' and 'Doer,' or rather the 'Player' and 'Dancer,' in the realm of created forms, of time, of history, of nature, of life.

"Conditioned brahman, then, appears in the world of nature and time under personal forms (various incarnations for Hinduism, one incarnation only for Christianity). Realization of the Supreme 'Player' whose 'play' (lila) is manifested in the million-formed inexhaustible richness of beings and events is what gives us the *key to the meaning of life. Once we live in awareness of the cosmic dance and move in time with the Dancer, our life attains its true dimensions* (emphasis mine). It is at once more serious and less serious than the life of one who does not sense this inner cosmic dynamism. To live without this illuminated consciousness is to live as a beast of burden, carrying one's life with tragic seriousness as a huge incomprehensible weight, (see Camus' interpretation of the myth of Sisyphus). The weight of the burden is the seriousness with which one takes one's own individual and separate self. To live with the true consciousness of life centered in Another is to lose one's self-important seriousness and thus to live life as 'play' in union with a Cosmic Player. It is He alone that one takes seriously.

But to take Him seriously is to find joy and spontaneity in everything, for everything is gift and grace. In other words to live selfishly is to bear life as an intolerable burden. To live selflessly is to live in joy, realizing by experience that life itself is love and gift. *To be a lover and a giver is to be a channel through which the Supreme Giver manifests His love in the world."*(Emphasis mine) by Thomas Merton, from THE ASIAN JOURNALS OF THOMAS MERTON. Copyright (1975 by The Trustees of the Merton Legacy Trust. Reprinted by permission of New Directions Publishing Corp. p. 349-350.

Recommended Reading

Blakney, Raymond B., trans. *Meister Eckhart* (New York: Harper & Row, 1941).

Bhagavad-Gita. Introduction by Aldous Huxley (New York: The New American Library, 1951).

Campbell, Joseph. *Historical Atlas of World Mythology*, Vol. I: Parts 1 and 2; Vol. II, Part 1 (New York: Harper & Row, 1988).

Campbell, Joseph. *The Inner Reaches of Outer Space* (New York, Harper & Row, 1986).

Chopra, Deepak. *Unconditional Life* (New York: Bantam Books, 1992).

Cousineau, Phil, ed. *The Hero's Journey: Joseph Campbell on His Life and Work* (New York: Harper & Row, 1990).

DeMello, Anthony. *Song of the Bird* (New York: Doubleday Pub. Co., 1984).

DeMello, Anthony. *Awareness* (New York: Doubleday Pub. Co., 1992).

Franck, Frederick. *The Book of Angelus Silesius* (New York: Random House, 1976).

Leroy, Pierre. *Letters from My Friend, Teilhard de Chardin*, trans. Mary Lucas (Ramsey, New Jersey: Paulist Press, 1976).

Merton, Thomas. *Asian Journal* (New York: New Directions Pub. Corp., 1973).

Merton, Thomas. *The Way of Chuang Tzu* (New York: New Directions Pub. Corp., 1969).

Milne, A. A. *The House at Pooh Corner* (New York: Dell Pub. Co., 1958).

Raub, John Jacob. *Who Told You That You Were Naked?* (New York: Crossroad, 1992).

Shea, John. *Starlight* (New York: Crossroad, 1992).

Some', Malidoma Patrice, *Of Water and the Spirit* (New York: Penguin Books, 1994).

Swimme, Brian. *The Universe is a Green Dragon* (Santa Fe, New Mexico: Bear & Co. Inc., 1984).

Swimme, Brian and Berry, Thomas, *The Universe Story* (San Francisco: Harper Collins, 1992).

Tao Te Ching, trans. Gia-Fu Feng and Jane English (New York: Random House, 1972).

Tao Te Ching, trans. Stephen Mitchell (Harper & Row, 1988).

Toolan, S.J., David. *Nature, a Hericlitian Fire* (St. Louis, MO. Studies in the Spirituality of Jesuits; Nov. 1991).

Weiss, M.D., Brian. *Many Lives, Many Masters* (New York: Simon & Schuster, Inc., 1988).

Zukav, Gary. *The Seat of the Soul* (New York: Simon & Schuster, Inc., 1990).